Introduction to Microeconomics

Dr. Heena Jagdishkumar Pandhi

(M.Com., M.Ed., Ph.D.)
Principal
Silver Bells Institute of Commerce (B.Com.)
Bhavnagar, Gujarat

Canadian Academic Publishing

2015

Price : $27.86

First Edition : 2015

ISBN : 978-1-926488-04-2

Publisher ISBN Prefix : 978-1-926488

ISBN Allotment Agency : Library and Archives Canada (Govt. of Canada)

Published & Printed by
Canadian Academic Publishing
81, Woodlot Crescent,
Etobicoke,
Toronto, Ontario, Canada.
Postal Code- M9W 6T3
Phone- +1 (647) 633 9712
http://www.canadapublish.com

Dedicated to:

My Parents

&

Students of Class XIIth (Commerce) of
Silver Bells Public School, Bhavnagar, Gujarat.

PREFACE

"HARD WORK AND INTELLEGENCE COMBINED WITH GOOD GUIDANCE LEADS TO SUCCESS"

It gives me immense pleasure to bring out a book on Introduction to Micro Economics which covers major theories related to Micro Economics.

Every effort has been made to explain the various economic concepts and theories in a simple and lucid style. The present Endeavour is an attempt to provide a reliable book in a comprehensive form for the readers of this book. The basic concepts of economics principles have been explained in simple words with familiar examples in tabular as well as graphical representation without sacrificing depth of the subject matter.

In the task of writing the present book I record my indebtedness to all who have extended their help and suggestions. I shall feel amply rewarding if the book is proved worthwhile for all those for whom it is written.

At this point, I would like to record my gratitude to my parents and family to help me reach to a destiny. I am also grateful to Dr. Kalyanji who inspired me in starting this work.

Lastly, but strongly I would like to dedicate this piece of work to my beloved students of class XIIth (Commerce) of Silver Bells Public School, Bhavnagar. Suggestions for further improvement of this book are welcome and shall be gratefully acknowledged.

Dr. Heena Jagdishkumar Pandhi

CONTENTS

Chapter - 1

Introduction to Micro Economics

In this Chapter you will clear your concepts about…..

➢ **Definition of Micro Economics**

➢ **Definition of Macro Economics**

➢ **Difference between Micro Economics and Macro Economics**

➢ **Similarities between Micro and Macro Economics**

➢ **What is an Economy?**

➢ **Types of Economy**

➢ **Central Problems of an Economy**

➢ **Basic Concept of Production Possibility Frontier or Production Frontier Curve or Transformation Curve**

➢ **Basic Concept of Opportunity Cost or Economic Cost**

Chapter - 1

Introduction to Micro Economics

1.1 Introduction

Economics is the social science studying the production, distribution and consumption of goods and services. It is a complex social science that spans from mathematics to psychology. At its most basic, however, economics considers how a society provides for its needs. Its most basic need is survival; which requires food, clothing and shelter. Once those are covered, it can then look at more sophisticated commodities such as services, personal transport, entertainment, the list goes on. Although there are other branches of Economic Studies, i.e. Micro and Macro Economics are the most well known economy used worldwide. These economics shared some of the same concepts and they are interrelated too. This economics deals with a simple economy where goods and services are bought and sold. Basic necessities of an individual are the key point.

1.2 Definition of Micro Economics

Micro economics looks at the behaviors of individual people and companies within the economy. It is the consumer whose demand is driving force behind the prices and production of particular goods or services. Micro economics deals with an individual firm or a company in the present economy. It deals with relationship between individual units of economy. Consumer behavior is essential in micro economics. The basic principle of micro economics is "Theory of the firm". Micro economics touches the factors of Demand, Supply, Price and Performance of particular commodity in the market.

1.3 Definition of Macro Economics

The term 'Macro' is derived from the Greek word, i.e. 'Macro' which means large. Macro economics look at their economy as the whole.

2

It examine the factors that determine national output and it's growth. It studies about 'Aggregate' which relates to the general prices, total employment income and production. In the word of Edward Shapiro, the major look of Macro economics is the explanation of what determines the economy in aggregate output of goods and services.

1.4 Difference between Micro Economics and Macro Economics

Basics	Micro Economics	Macro Economics
Scope	Micro economics studies the problems of individual, firm or unit.	Macro economics studies the problems of or related to group or whole economy.
Objective	It studies the problem of prices, resources, allocation etc.	It studies the problem of economic growth, employment, income, etc.
Determinacy	The main determinant of micro economics is price.	The main determinant of macro economics is national income.
Approach	It refers to basic or individual demand following with it's supply.	It refers to average or aggregate of the whole group concerned.

1.5 Similarities between Micro and Macro Economics

Micro and Macro economics deals with theories and practices of economy. Both the theories of economy deals with individual behavior in the market. Micro and Macro economics refers to the economics problems of the country. Micro as well as Macro economics answers the questions related to demand, supply, output as well as price factor. Micro and Macro economics also understand the conditions of the market which is prevailing at the presence. These economics are interrelated to each other as group of individual get together and form Macro and if separated turns into Micro. These two are two side of a one coin, where micro economics is the beginning and macro economics is towards its end.

3

1.6   What is an Economy?

An economy is a type of situation, where one who needs, meets the one who sells. Economy is a situation where the basic necessities of a consumer is been satisfied and he/she pays for the same. A consumer is said to be the king of the market. It is the consumer who satisfies their needs and wants in form of goods and services; they pay for the same in minority form. They satisfy their basic necessities such as food, clothes, shelter, and basic services. Every individual is included in this economy.

1.7   Types of Economy

Mainly there are two types of economy which are as follows:

1. The Centrally Planned Economy :

In this type of economy, Government plans every economic activity, decision regarding production, consumption and exchange of goods and services with money. It is decided by the government. The centrally planned economy is under the control of government.

2. The Market Economy :

In this type of economy, the conditions are in the hand of the market. In this economy the consumer is said to be the king. It is the individual who decides everything. In this economy buyers and sellers interact with each other for buying and selling of commodities and services. Buyers and sellers interacts with each other by face to face, telephonic discussion and through internet. During this interaction, positive and negative aspects of products and services are discussed.

1.8   Central Problems of an Economy

When an individual or group of people enters into an economy, the first things that click in their mind are which problem they will face in a

4

market while entering it. The seller or producer faces mainly three central problem of an economy.

A. What is to be produce?
B. How to produce?
C. For whom to produce?

Let us discuss these central problems in details.

A. What is to be Produce?

The seller or producer faces this type of problem at the very initial stage while entering in an economy. What to be produce? This is one of the question to be answer. Whether to produce a commodity which satisfies the basic necessities and wants of a consumer or whether to produce agriculture product or an industrial product. Whether the goods produce will be of luxuries type or not in one of question that arises in the mind of the producer which services to produce, i.e. health services, transportation, education services etc is to be decided under this central problem.

B. How to Produce?

The second central problem face by the producer in an economy is how to produce? Under such circumstances the producer after getting the answer what to produce will think over how to produce it?. Which technique will the seller or the producer use while producing that product? Whether labor intensive technique can be used? is decided over here. More of man power to use or use machine-intensive technology to be used. If the producer decides to machine-intensive technology what capital will be invested is decided. New technologies can be adopted or not is decided under this question.

C. For Whom to Produce?

In this central problem the seller or the producer makes a decision that the product which are produced will be utilized by whom ?, Whether these goods will be consumed by people residing in urban or rural area ?, Whether these goods will be allocated to places were scarcity is there ?, Will these commodity be consumed by someone who is in need ?. The producer tries to solve out these central problems by carrying out a small and simple Survey.

When economy is discussed the above stated problems are to be kept in mind and a producer can interact with the consumer and discuss these problems.

1.9 Basic Concept of Production Possibility Frontier or Production Frontier Curve or Transformation Curve

The curve which shows the various alternatives production combination of goods that can be produced with given resources and technology, such type of possibility is known as Production Possibility Frontier (PPF). In such type of situation, the resources which are scare are fully and effectively utilized. The best alternative usage is opted over here. How to allocate resources which are limited is practiced here. Let us understand with an example along with a schedule and a graph. An economy which can produce only two goods that is Rice and Sugar the quantity is as follows:

Rice	Sugar
10	35
20	30
30	20
40	10

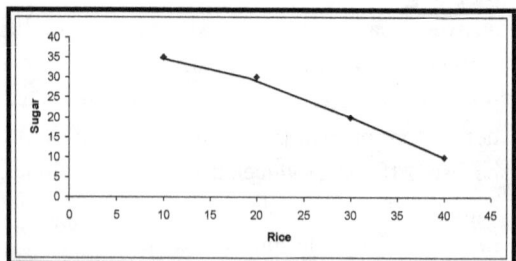

Explanation of the Curve / Graph

One assumption that in an economy, a producer can produce maximum sixty (60) units only. According to this the combination which a producer can produce that is production possibility is as under:

- Set A :- 20 units of Rice and 30 units of Sugar

- Set B :- 30 units of Rice and 20 units of Sugar

- Set C :- 40 units of Rice and 10 units of Sugar

- But a producer can not produce 30 units of Rice and 35 units of Sugar. As the maximum possibility is 60 units only.

1.10 Basic Concept of Opportunity Cost or Economic Cost

Opportunity cost is the cost of next best alternative forgone. This opportunity cost is applicable to an individual as well as the whole society. Opportunity cost is the cost of any good which is been sacrificed for the other goods. For e.g. A farmer can cultivate Wheat and Potato in his farm using the same factor of production. The opportunities cost can be determined as follows:

i)   100 Kg of Wheat fetches Rs. 1000

ii)   100 Kg of Potatoes fetches Rs. 1500

If a farmer selects Potatoes to be cultivated in his farm the opportunity cost of this farming would be Rs. 1000 (As Wheat is sacrificed).

1.11 Question Bank

1. Define micro economics.

2. Define macro economics.

3. Differentiate between micro and macro economics.

4. Compare micro and macro economics.

5. Explain the concept of economy and discuss its type.

6. State the central problems of an economy.

7. Explain the concept of production possibility curve with a graph.

8. What is opportunity cost? Explain with an example.

Chapter - 2

Consumer Equilibrium and Utility

In this Chapter you will clear your concepts about…..

- *Concept of Equilibrium*
- *Meaning of Consumer Equilibrium*
- *Concept of Utility*
- *Types of Utility*
- *Relation between Total Utility (Tu) and Marginal Utility (Mu)*
- *Measurement of Utility*
- *Introduction to Law of Diminishing Marginal Utility*
- *Diminishing Marginal Utility Schedule and Curve / Graph*
- *Conditions of Consumer Equilibrium using Mu Analysis*
- *Conditions of consumer equilibrium*

Chapter - 2

Consumer Equilibrium and Utility

2.1   Introduction

All consumers strive to maximize their utility. We try to get as much satisfaction as we can. The consumer's scale of preference is derived by means of indifference mapping that is a set of indifference curves which ranks the preferences of the consumer. Getting to the indifference curve which is far from the origin gives the highest total utility. Although the goal of the consumer is maximization of satisfaction, the means of achieving the goal is not clear. Higher indifference curve not only gives higher satisfaction but also are more expensive. Here we are confronted with the basic conflict between preferences and the prices of the commodities consumer wants to consume. With a given amount of money income to spent, we cannot attain the highest satisfaction but have to settle for less.

2.2   Concept of Equilibrium

When a consumer enters in the market he enters with demands in his mind for specific commodities. Let those commodities be consumer goods, basic necessities goods or any luxuries product. When a consumer wishes to buy these things then most essential part is his purchasing power. His income is an important aspect in a market. When a consumer purchases goods at a price which is affordable and being supplied in a market, where his satisfaction is highest. Such situation in terms of economics is said to be equilibrium.

Equilibrium is such type of circumstances when a consumer's demand is fully satisfied by the supply of a commodity at a reasonable price. Here, a consumer has no tendency to change his wants as it is satisfied. Maximum satisfaction point is obtained.

2.3 Meaning of Consumer Equilibrium

When a consumer in a market is highly satisfied with the goods and services supplied by the producer at an affordable price (i.e. less than income) that particular point is said to be consumer equilibrium. When a consumer reaches at this point, his allocation of money is positive. No need to re-allocate his income in purchasing other goods. At this point, no changes in need, want, demand, and supply are desired.

2.4 Concept of Utility

Anything which satisfies a human wants directly or indirectly is known as utility. A utility of product is satisfying the human wants which arises. Utility can be termed as "Wants Satisfaction Power". Quality which is desirable and expectable is being achieved and consumed is said as utility. Ability of goods to satisfy a wants is termed as utility. Utility is a power of satisfying a wants only if it is consumed. A mere desire to purchase a good cannot be termed as utility. It needs to be consumed by the consumer.

2.5 Types of Utility

Utility is classified as follows :

A. Total Utility (Tu)

B. Marginal Utility (Mu)

A. Total Utility (Tu)

Total utility means sum of total of utility derived from the consumption of all units of a commodity. In simple words, when a need or want is satisfied by consuming a particular commodity, one by one in units and the sum of total of these consumptions is known as Total Utility. Symbolically, it is notified as 'Tu'. The formulae of total utility is,

$U_1 + U_2 + U_3 \ldots\ldots U_n$

Where 'n' denotes the last units of consumed.

B. Marginal Utility (Mu)

Marginal utility is the addition made to the total utility by consuming one more unit of a commodity. Marginal utility is results from a units increase in consumption. Symbolically, it denoted as 'Mu'. Mu is the one more unit that is consume and added up to total utility. Thus it can be said that the excess unit consumed beyond Tu.

2.6 Relation between Total Utility (Tu) and Marginal Utility (Mu)

The relationship between Total Utility (Tu) and Marginal Utility (Mu) can be easily defined with this example,

Quantity	Total Utility (Tu)	Marginal Utility (Mu)
1	10	10 – Initial
2	18	8 – (18-10)
3	24	6 – (24-18)
4	28	4 – (28-24)
5	30	2 – (30-28)
6	30	0 – (30-30)
7	28	-2 – (28-30)

The relationship between Tu and Mu is as under:

- When Tu increases, Mu stays positive
- When Tu is at maximum Mu = 0
- When Tu decreases, Mu start turns towards negative slope.

Every addition of units increases marginal utility which changes from positive to negative.

2.7 Measurement of Utility

Utility in real sense cannot be measured. Utility is something which is immeasurable but further let us classify it into two types of measurements.

A.   Cardinal Utility

B.   Ordinal Utility

A. Cardinal Utility

Cardinal utility means the utility which can measure in units / utile, which is later converted into prices of that commodity. Cardinal utility is measured in terms of money. For e.g. 1 Apple = Rs. 10, therefore apple worth Rs. 10 is cardinal utility measured.

B. Ordinal Utility

Ordinal utility means when a particular commodity is measured in terms of units / utile. For e.g. 1 apple, 2 apples, 3 apples and so on.

2.8 Introduction to Law of Diminishing Marginal Utility

In economics, the marginal utility of a good or service is the gain from an increase, or loss from a decrease, in the consumption of that good or service. Economists sometimes speak of a law of diminishing marginal utility, meaning that the first unit of consumption of a good or service yields more utility than the second and subsequent units, with a continuing reduction for greater amounts. The marginal decision rule states that a good or service should be consumed at a quantity at which the marginal utility is equal to the marginal cost. The law of diminishing marginal utility is similar to the law of diminishing returns which states that as the amount of one factor of production increases as all other factors of production are held the same, the marginal return (extra output gained by adding an extra unit) decreases.

2.9 Definition of Law of Diminishing Marginal Utility

"The additional benefits which a person derives from a given increase of his stock of things, diminishes with every increase in the stock that he already had.

- Prof. Alfred Marshall

2.10 Explanation of Law of Diminishing Marginal Utility

Law of diminishing marginal utility states that when a particular person adds the consumption of the commodity beyond total utility he had it is known as marginal utility of that commodity. Marginal utility of that commodity goes an decreasing as more units are consumed. 'More intake of goods = Fall of marginal utility'.

Here it's important facts:

- Total wants of a man are unlimited and every want is satisfactory.
- Different goods are not perfect substitution for each other.

2.11 Diminishing Marginal Utility Schedule and Curve / Graph

Let us understand Diminishing Marginal Utility with the help if schedule and graph.

(Schedule) Cup of Tea	Total Utility (Tu)	Marginal Utility (Mu)
1	12	12 – Initial
2	22	10 – (22-12)
3	30	8 – (30-22)
4	36	6 – (36-30)
5	40	4 – (40-36)
6	41	1 – (41-40)
7	39	-2 – (39-41)
8	34	-5 – (34-39)

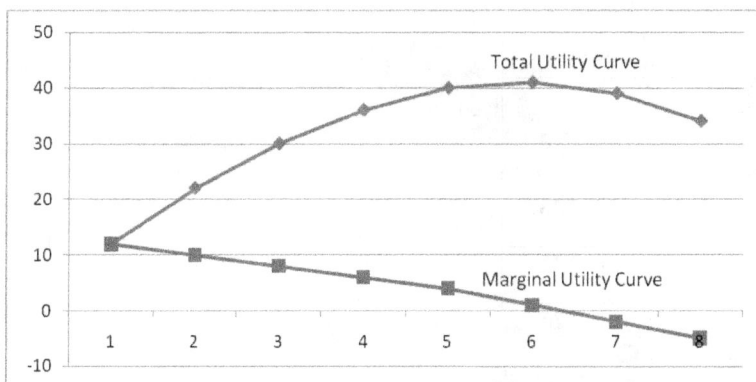

Explanation of the Curve / Graph

From the above graph a clear picture of diminishing marginal utility is observed. It can be noticed that increase in units leads to decrease in marginal utility, which in turn be zero (0) and further going towards the negative marginal utility.

2.12 Assumptions of the Law of Diminishing Marginal Utility

Assumptions of the Law of Diminishing Marginal Utility are as follows:

- The consumer should be rational.
- All commodities should be homogeneous.
- No time interval should be given.
- Price, Habit, Taste, Preference and Income remains constant.

2.13 Conditions of Consumer Equilibrium using Mu Analysis

Consumer equilibrium is when given income and market prices he / she plans his / her expenditure in such a way that maximizes the total satisfaction. Let us understand with a schedule and a graph.

Unit	Mu	Price
1	40	25
2	35	25
3	30	25
4	**25**	**25**
5	20	25
6	15	25

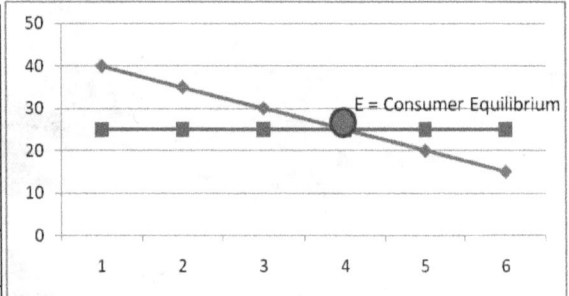

E = Consumer Equilibrium

Explanation of the Curve / Graph

As observed from the above graph, unit 4 is a point of intersection of Mu line and price line, which is denoted as 'E', i.e. consumer equilibrium. This point defines that a consumer is highly satisfied when Mu=P.

2.14 Conditions of consumer equilibrium

The conditions of consumer equilibrium using Mu analysis are as follows:

1. The consumer should be rational.
2. Price of a commodity remains stable.
3. Measurement of utility must be possible in form of satisfaction.
4. Consumer should purchase that much quantity of that commodity so that Marginal utility of a commodity is equal to its price.

2.15 Question Bank

1. Explain the concept of equilibrium.

2. What do you mean by utility? Discuss its types.

3. State the relationship between Tu and Mu.

4. How can utility be measured?

5. Describe Law of Diminishing Marginal Utility with a graph.

6. State the conditions of consumer equilibrium.

Chapter - 3

Consumer Budget

In this Chapter you will clear your concepts about…..

- ➢ *Concept of Consumer Budget*
- ➢ *Budget Set*
- ➢ *Change in Budget Set*
- ➢ *Budget Line*
- ➢ *Point below and above the Budget Line*
- ➢ *Price ratio and slope of Budget Line*
- ➢ *Preference of the consumers*
- ➢ *Monotonic Preference*
- ➢ *Diminishing Rate of Substitution or Convex Preference*
- ➢ *Indifference Curve*
- ➢ *Point below and above the Indifference Curve*
- ➢ *An Indifference Map*
- ➢ *Substitute and Slope of Indifference Curve*
- ➢ *Conditions of Consumer Equilibrium at Indifference Curve*

Chapter - 3

Consumer Budget

3.1 Introduction

A person who enters a market with an intension to spend money to purchase a commodity which can satisfy his wants and demand is known as a "consumer". A consumer purchases goods and services for its utility. But when he enters in a market, he has some common points in his mind, such as:

1. What best commodity can he be satisfied with?

2. Are there any close substitutes of that particular commodity available in the market?

3. What best bargain price can he pay for that product?

The above questions always click his mind before purchasing a commodity. But above all, one of the most important question that needs to be solved is: How much will he spend for each and every product he purchases?

3.2 Concept of Consumer Budget

Consumer has fixed amount of income to spend. In this, he has to purchase more than one commodity for satisfying his daily needs. Every commodity at a given price is not possible to purchase. Therefore, he will try to make combinations of those products whose cost is less, or equal to his income. This is known as "Consumer Budget"

3.3 Budget Set

Budget set is a quantitative combination of those products which a consumer can purchase from his given income at a prevailing market price. For a budget sets, combinations of products are made.

- X_1 and X_2 are the goods or the commodity.
- P_1 and P_2 are the price of that goods or the commodity.
- M is the income of the consumers.

According to this, to purchase a product or a commodity X_1 a consumer will have to pay P_1. Therefore, $P_1 X_1$ is to be kept in mind. Same for the second product X_2. To purchase a product or a commodity X_2 a consumer will have to pay P_2. Therefore, $P_2 X_2$ is to be kept in mind. Here P_1X_1 and P_2X_2 are called as Budget Set. But these budget set should be less than or equal to the income of the consumer.

Therefore, $P_1X_1 + P_2X_2 \leq M$.

3.4 Change in Budget Set

Due to one or the other reasons, there can be increase or decrease in the income of the consumers. These changes of income is denoted by M'. Due to change in income, there is a change in budget set. There are two possibilities for a change in a budget set. These possibilities are as follows:

Possibility No. 1 When M' changes

As the income of the consumer changes, change in budget set is observed. Either income increases or can decrease. Therefore, $P_1X_1 + P_2X_2 = M'$. Two cases can be discussed here:

Case 1: When income decreases

When income decreases, the graph shows downward slope according to it. Let us understand it with a schedule and a graph.

Income	X
20	20
15	10

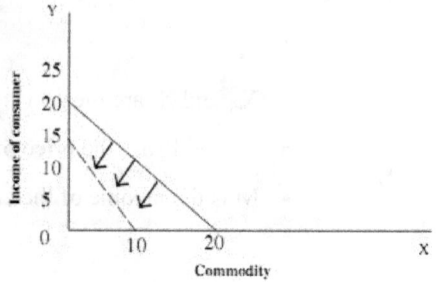

Explanation of the Curve / Graph

It is clear from the above graph that when the income of the consumer decreases, the purchasing power of the consumers tends to decrease. Therefore when M decreases the graph shows a downward slope. Here M' is less than M.

Case 2: When income increases

When income increases, the graph shows upward slope according to it. Let us understand it with a schedule and a graph.

P₁	P₂
20	20
30	30

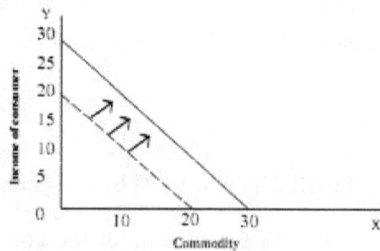

Explanation of the Curve / Graph

It is clear from the above graph that when the income of the consumer increases, the purchasing power of the consumers tends to increase. Therefore when M increases the graph shows a upward slope. Here M' is greater than M.

Possibility No. 2   Change in price of one product

When the income of the consumers remains constant along with the change in the price of one commodity, budget set also observes a change. Two cases can be discussed here:

Case 1: When price of the product decreases

When income and price of the other commodity remains constant with decrease in price of one commodity is seen, budget set observes a change. Let us understand it with a schedule and a graph.

Price	X
20	20
20	30

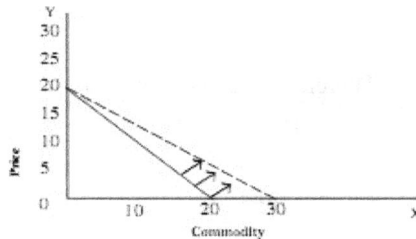

Explanation of the Curve / Graph

It is clear from the above graph that when the income and price of second product remains constant and decrease in one commodity is observed the budget set of the consumer will also change respectively.

Case 2: When price of the product Increases

When income and price of the other commodity remains constant with a increase in price of one commodity is seen, budget set observes a change. Let us understand it with a schedule and a graph.

Price	X
20	20
20	10

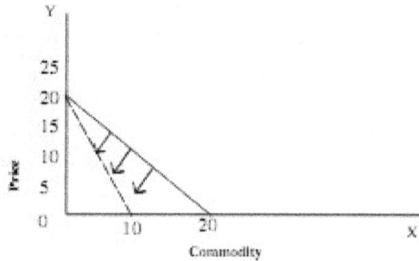

Explanation of the Curve / Graph

It is clear from the above graph that when the income and price of second product remains constant and increase in one commodity is observed the budget set of the consumer will also change respectively.

Therefore, it can be said that $P_1'X_1 + P_2X_2 = M$

3.5   Budget Line

Budget line shows all those combinations of commodity which a consumer can buy by spending his income on those commodity which can satisfy them the most in the given price.

According to Hibbins, "The budget line shows all the different combinations of two commodities that a consumer can purchase in his income and the price prevailing in the market."

The Budget line consists of all bundles which is exactly equal to his income. i.e. M. Therefore, $P_1X_1 + P_2X_2 = M$. When both the commodities are perfectly equal to income, A budget line is formed. Let us understand it with a schedule and a graph.

Budget Line

P₁	P₂
10	30
20	**20**
30	10

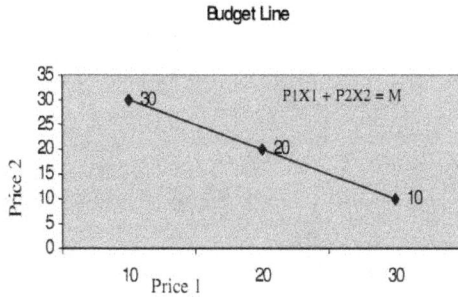

Explanation of the Curve / Graph

It is clear from the above graph that when the prices of both the commodities are equal to the income of a consumer, A budget line is observed diagonally in the graph.

3.6 Point below and above the Budget Line

The diagram indicates budget line. Any point outside or inside this budget line shows that a consumer is either not able to spend money on purchase of the commodity or is not interested in spending any amount to get those goods.

When a point lies below the budget line, this point is known as point below the budget line. Here a schedule and graph can be presented to show point below the budget line.

P₁	P₂
30	0
20	15
10	25
0	30

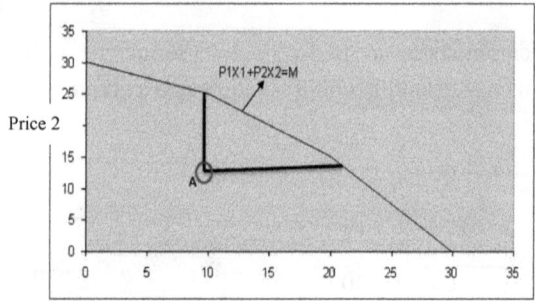

Price 1

Explanation of the Curve / Graph

Here, point A lies under the budget line which indicates that a consumer with given income and price of a product P_1 and P_2 purchases a product, but point A is in such a position that consumer will have a left over (excess amount) income and can utilize for other purposes. This is called as point below budget line.

When a point lies above the budget line, this point is known as point above the budget line. Here a schedule and graph can be presented to show point above the budget line.

P₁	P₂
30	0
20	15
10	25
0	30

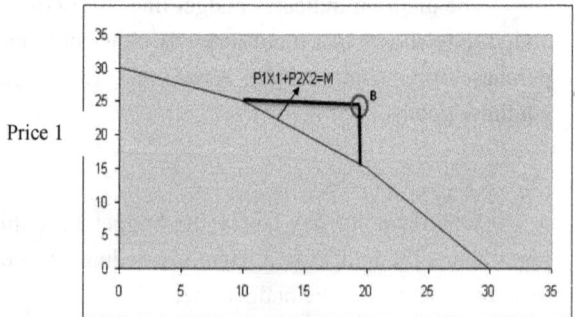

Price 2

26

Explanation of the Curve / Graph

Here, point B lies above the budget line which indicates that a consumer with given income and price of a product P_1 and P_2 purchases a product, but point B is in such a position that the purchase of commodities are out of reach with reference to the income of the consumer. So consumer is not able to purchase that particular commodity at that point. This is called as point above budget line.

3.7 Price ratio and slope of Budget Line

When a price ratio changes, slope of budget line also changes. This is because of effect of change in income of the consumers and prices of the commodities. There are two possibilities in price ratio. They are as follows:

1. If the price of the product X increases the quantity purchased within the income will fall, and result into shift of budget line to the left side.

2. If the prices of the commodities decrease, quantity purchased will increase. If the price of the product X increases, a consumer will have to scarifies the second product quantity wise. Therefore, X for Y will be substituted with the reason change in price that is P_1 and P_2.

3.8 Preference of the consumers

When a consumer thinks to purchase any goods or commodity or any services at prevailing price in a market, his thinking depends upon his choice and preference. A consumer will always wish that the commodity that he purchases should satisfy his needs and wants the most. Choice of a particular product totally depends upon the consumer's wish. There are reasons which lead to a particular selection of a product. These reasons can be his taste, habit, preference, budget, substitute, price factor, its alternative usage etc.

When more than one commodity is to be preferred, the consumer builds sets of preferences in his mind. Set preference means combination of two commodities at a given price in the limits of the consumer's income. These sets can be symbolically be denoted as X_1, X_2 or Y_1, Y_2.

3.9 Monotonic Preference

When a consumer first prefers a set of commodity, suppose X_1, X_2; later with several reasons such as taste, habit, preference, budget, substitute, price factor, its alternative usage etc. changes to product Y_1, Y_2, This shift of preference is termed as monotonic preference.

For monotonic preference, the consumer should get the best substitute of present commodities preferred. If he gets the best substitutes, then and then only he will shift his preferences. This change is denoted by Δ and pronounced as DELTA. For example, the commodity set preferred are (1, 2) & (2, 1). Now Set 1 is the first preference, if a consumer from Set 1 wants one product changed with Set 2 then that is known as change in preference set. The rate of substitution for a product should be 1:1.

3.10 Diminishing Rate of Substitution or Convex Preference

When price of a commodity increases, a buyer cannot afford more of second commodity in a fix parameter of his income. This is called as diminishing rate of substitution. In a given pre-determined income of the consumer when he has to choose a product or go in for a monotonic preference, he will have to sacrifice one of the products to gain that particular product. This is also termed as convex preference. Let us understand with a schedule and a graph.

X_1	X_2
5	25
10	20
15	15
20	10
25	5

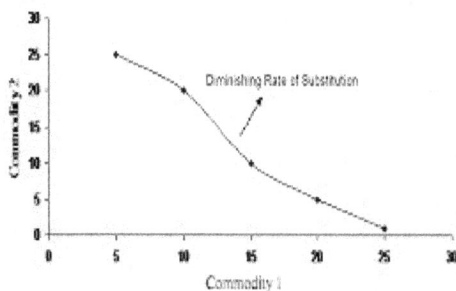

Explanation of the Curve / Graph

From the above graph it is clear that when the price of a product increases gradually the consumer with a fixed income has to decrease the consumption of another commodity. This is known as diminishing rate of substitution or convex preference as the graph is convex to its origin.

3.11 Indifference Curve

An indifference curve is the locus of points particularly combinations of goods that yield same utility to a consumer so that he is indifferent as to the particular combination. The consumer indifference curve is a curve which represents all those combinations of the commodity which gives same satisfaction to the consumers. Since all the combinations on an indifference curve give the same satisfaction, the consumer is indifferent among themselves. This curve is also known as "ISO Utility Curve".

According to Mayers, "An indifference curve may be defined as a schedule of various combinations of commodities of goods which may be equally satisfactory to the consumer concerned." Let us understand with a schedule and a graph.

X_1	X_2
1	12
2	8
3	5
4	3
5	2

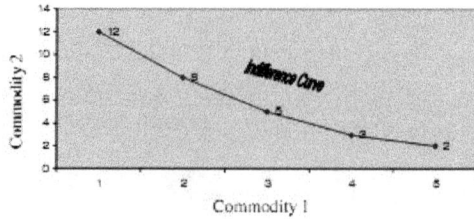

Explanation of the Curve / Graph

From the above graph it is clear that indifference curve being locus of points of particular commodities or bundles of goods which provides same level of satisfaction to the consumer. But, it is clear that as a consumer if commodity X_1 is demanded more, commodity X_2 is to be sacrificed. This is called Marginal Rate of Substitution" (MRS) or can be named as slope of indifference curve. When comparison of two products are done symbolically it is denoted as

$$MRS = \frac{\Delta X_2}{\Delta X_1}$$

3.12 Assumption of Indifference Curve

1. The consumer should be rational.

2. Consumer has monotonic preference.

3. Price of goods and income of the consumer are pre-determined.

4. There will be no change in the taste and preference of the consumer at a regular interval.

3.13 Properties of Indifference Curve

The properties of the indifference curve are as follows:

1. Slope of indifference curve

A slope of indifference curve will always slope from left to right direction. If a consumer increases one unit of a particular commodity, other one has to be decreases.

2. Convex to its origin

A shape of indifference curve is always convex to its origin. This is due to Marginal Rate of Substitution (MRS). That is the reason why indifference curve will never intersect each other as it has its own level of satisfaction.

3. Level of satisfaction.

Higher indifference curve represents higher level of satisfaction. This is because combinations on the graph contains more of satisfaction fo one or both the commodities.

3.14 Point below and above the Indifference Curve

When a consumer selects a set of bundles of commodities, the best way of getting satisfied is his main goal. When two bundles of set is to be taken into consideration, let it say X_1 and X_2 = A and Y_1 and Y_2 = B, then in this situation when a consumer prefers set which lies on point C, it is said to be a superior selection. Whereas when a consumer prefers set which lies on point D, it is said to be a inferior selection. Let us understand with a schedule and a graph.

P₁	P₂
5	12
8	6
12	4

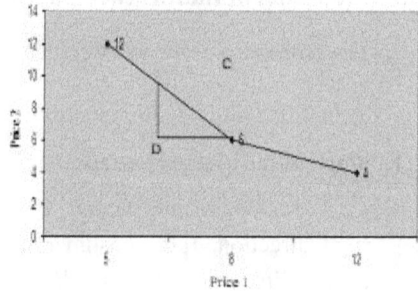

Explanation of the Curve / Graph

From the above graph it is clear that when in a situation where a consumer prefers a set which lies on point C, it is said to be a superior selection. Whereas when a consumer prefers a set which lies on point D, it is said to be a inferior selection. This shows point above and below the indifference curve.

3.15 An Indifference Map

A set of indifference curves is called indifference map. An indifference map shows all the indifferent curves which ranks the preference of the consumers. Combination of goods situated on an indifference curve possesses same utility.

An indifference map therefore figures out complete picture of consumer's taste and preferences. An indifference map is like a counter line on a map which shows the level of satisfaction of a consumer. Let us understand with a graph.

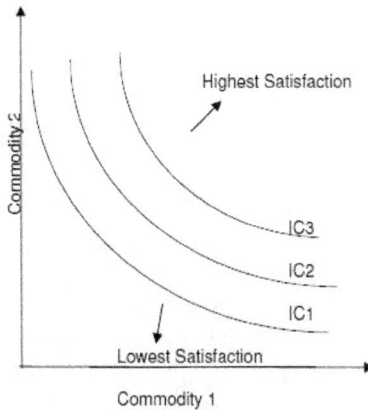

Commodity 2 (vertical axis)

Highest Satisfaction

IC3
IC2
IC1

Lowest Satisfaction

Commodity 1

Explanation of the Curve / Graph

From the above graph it is clear that IC_1 is the lowest satisfied bundle of commodities for a consumer whereas that IC_3 is the highest satisfied bundle of commodities for a consumer.

3.16 Substitute and Slope of Indifference Curve

As a consumer is willing to satisfy his needs every time, he goes on for monotonic preferences i.e. shift of choice in products in a given income. The first preference can be stated as X_1 and X_2 which is later on shifted to ΔX_1 and ΔX_2 with the concept of monotonic preference. Let us understand with a schedule and a graph.

X_1	X_2
1	12
2	8
3	5
4	3
5	2

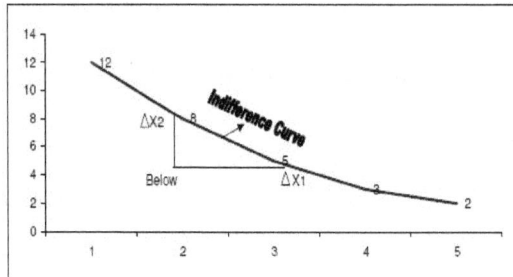

Explanation of the Curve / Graph

From the above graph it is clear that when a consumer shifts the choice of a product from X_1 and X_2 which is shifted to ΔX_1 and ΔX_2 the slope of indifference curve shifts downward.

3.17 Conditions of Consumer Equilibrium at Indifference Curve

Keeping in mind the concept of indifference curve, analysis of consumer equilibrium it is clear that when a consumer reaches to the maximum satisfaction consumer equilibrium is gained. There is no possibility to make rearrangement o f purchases. The taste, preference and choice is satisfied. The optimum (most preferred) bundle would be on the budget line. Budget Set is well organized and highest level of indifference curve is observed.

The conditions for consumer equilibrium are as follows:

1. A consumer has fixed income and money to spend completely on goods selected. i.e. set of commodities.
2. The price of those set of commodities are fixed.
3. Commodities should be homogeneous.
4. Budget line should be equal to indifference curve.
5. Indifference curve should be convex to the point of origin at equilibrium point.

Let us understand with a graph.

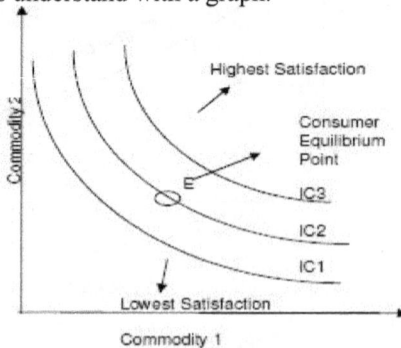

34

Explanation of the Curve / Graph

From the above graph it is clear that IC_1 is the lowest satisfied bundle of commodities for a consumer whereas that IC_3 is the highest satisfied bundle of commodities for a consumer. The IC_3 in this graph represents the equilibrium point. At this curve the consumer is highly satisfied with the purchase that he have done with his parameter of income he have with him.

3.18 Question Bank

1. Define
    a. Consumer Budget
    b. Budget Set
    c. Budget Line
    d. Monotonic Preference
2. State the possibilities of change in budget set.
3. Explain point below and above budget line.
4. State the possibilities in price ratio and slope of a budget line.
5. What is preference of a consumer?
6. What is convex preference?
7. Explain indifference curve with help of a diagram.
8. State the properties of indifference curve.
9. Explain point below and above indifference curve.
10. Explain indifference map.
11. Discuss the slope of indifference curve.
12. State the conditions of consumer equilibrium at indifference curve.

Chapter - 4

Demand and Elasticity of Demand

In this Chapter you will clear your concepts about.....

- ➤ *Concept of Demand*
- ➤ *Definition of Demand*
- ➤ *Law of Demand*
- ➤ *Demand Schedule and Demand Curve*
- ➤ *Market Demand*
- ➤ *Factors determining demand OR Factors affecting demand OR Determinants of demand*
- ➤ *Demand Function*
- ➤ *Variations in Demand*
- ➤ *Reasons for increase in Demand*
- ➤ *Reasons for decrease in Demand*
- ➤ *Distinguish between Quantity Demanded and Change in Demand*
- ➤ *Price Elasticity of Demand*
- ➤ *Degree / Kind of Elasticity of Demand*
- ➤ *Measurement of Price Elasticity of Demand*
- ➤ *Calculations of Price Elasticity of Demand*

Chapter - 4

Demand and Elasticity of Demand

4.1   Introduction

Demand is a buyer's willingness and ability to pay a price for a specific quantity of a good or service. Demand refers to how much (quantity) of a product or service is desired by buyers at various prices. The quantity demanded is the amount of a product people are willing to buy at a certain price; the relationship between price and quantity demanded is known as the demand. The term demand signifies the ability or the willingness to buy a particular commodity at a given point of time. Demand is the want or desire to possess goods or services with the necessary goods, services, or financial instruments necessary to make a legal transaction for those goods or services. The amount of a particular economic good or service that a consumer or group of consumers will want to purchase at a given price. Demand for a good or service is determined by many different factors other than price, such as the price of substitute goods and complementary goods.

4.2   Concept of Demand

Economically, when said "Demand" it means purchasing of a commodity and creates its utility. There is a vast difference between desire, wants and demand. Desire means idea or thoughts to possess it. Just having an idea or thought does not mean demand. When a consumer sacrifices other means to fulfill a desired is termed as "Wants". Whereas that consumer with the desire and wants purchase a commodity and consume it is termed as demand.

4.3   Definition of Demand

"The demand for any commodity is the relationship between price and the quantity that will be purchased at that price."

-      Waugh

"The demand for anything at a given price is the amount of it which will be brought per unit of time at that price. "

- Prof. Benham

4.4 Law of Demand

According to the law of demand, "Other things being stable or equal if the price of a commodity fall, the quantity demanded of it will rise and if the price of a commodity rises the quantity demanded will decline."

- Prof. Alfred Marshall

Therefore it can be said that when prices increased demand decreases and when the prices decreases demand increases. There is an inverse relationship between price and demand.

4.5 Demand Schedule and Demand Curve

Demand schedule is a tabular form of presentation for presenting the data for the demand and price of a commodity. Whereas this tabular form when graphically presented is said to be a Demand Curve.

Price	Quantity
1	12
2	8
3	5
4	3
5	2

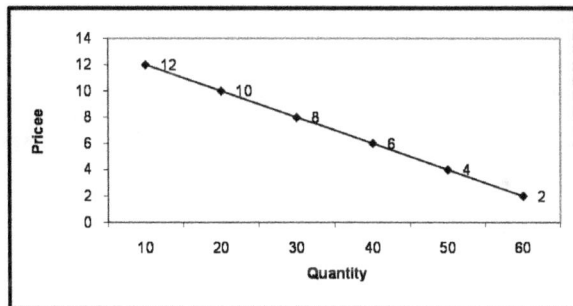

Explanation of the Curve / Graph

From the above demand curve it is clearly noticed that when a price of a commodity decreases the demand for that particular commodity decreases. Similarly when the price of a commodity increases the demand for that particular commodity increases.

4.6   Market Demand

The quantities of a given commodity which all consumers will buy at all possible prices at a given moment of time are known as market demand. Market demand refers to the sum total of the quantities demanded by all the individual households in the market by various price in given period of time.

Price	Commodity A	Commodity B	Commodity (A+B)
20	5	5	10
15	8	12	20
10	18	12	30
5	25	15	40

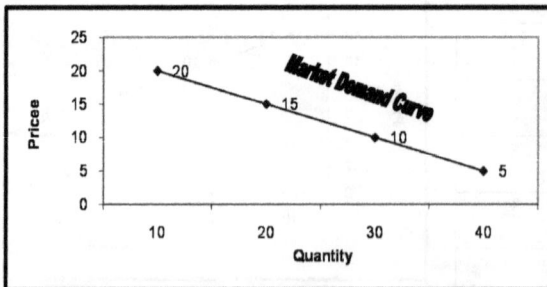

40

Explanation of the Curve / Graph

From the above graph it can be clearly noticed that the market demand curve is established by keeping in calculation with individual demand of the commodity A & B. A graph can be jointly represented as follows:

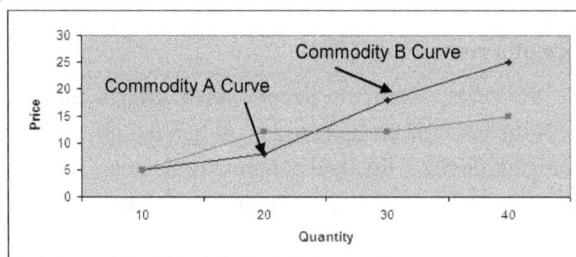

4.7   Assumption of the Law of Demand

- No change in price of the related goods.
- No change in income of the consumers.
- No change in taste and preference of consumers.
- No change in the price of that particular commodity.
- No change in population (number of consumers)
- No change in technology and discovery should be introduced.
- No change in weather and climate.

4.8   Exceptions of the Law of Demand.

- The giffen goods will not be affected by this law.
- The necessary goods will not be affected by this law.
- Emergency goods will not be affected by this law.
- Prestigious products will not be affected by this law.
- Scares commodity will not be affected by this law.

4.9 Factors determining demand OR Factors affecting demand OR Determinants of demand

The factors that affect demand in a market are related to consumers or the commodity part. The determinants of demand or factors affecting demand can be stated as follows:

1. Price of a commodity (Px)

One the most important factor which affects the demand in a market is the price of the commodity. When the price of a commodity increases the demand for that commodity decreases. Similarly when the price falls demand will rise. (Refer Law of Demand.

2. Price of related commodity (P$_R$)

Price of a related goods means the price of a substitute goods. If the price of the substitute goods will increase the demand for the original product will increase. Same way if the price of the substitute goods decreases the demand for the original product tends to decrease. Therefore there is a positive relationship between demand of the product and the price related to the commodity.

3. Price of a complementary commodity (Pc)

The price of complementary goods affects demand. When the price of complementary goods affects increases the demand of the main commodity is affected. As well a when the price of a complementary goods decrease demand increases. For example, Petrol is complementary goods for vehicles same ways ink is the complementary goods for pen.

4. Income of the consumers (Y)

Income of consumers affects demand. When there is a rise in income of consumers, the purchasing power of consumers increases which in returns affects demand positively. Similarly due to any reason if the income of the consumer decreases the demand in the market will be adversely affected.

5. Change in taste (T)

Change in taste, preference, habits or choice of a commodity highly influences demand. When a consumer changes its taste the demand of the product will decrease. Same way when there is no change in taste and preference the demand will remain constant or may even increase with more consumption.

6. Number of consumers (Population) (P)

The number of consumers affects the demand. More the consumers the rise in demand of a commodity is noticed. Whereas when the number of consumers declines the demand for that commodity also declines simultaneously. There is a positive relationship between the number of consumers and demand.

7. Climate and Season (C)

The consumer demands a product as per the climate and the seasons pertaining. The commodity necessary for a particular climate and season is demanded more. Whereas that particular commodity is not demanded in other seasons. Therefore the climate and season affects the demand.

8. Future expectation (F)

A consumer always keeps doubt of benefits. It means the consumer tries to build future expectations regarding price rise, shortage of goods etc. Due to this reason the consumer will start demanding for the more commodities which in turn influences demand.

9. Future Trends (FT)

The future trend is always judged by the consumers. Consumers have an habit of predictions. They predict future trends frequently. This is one of the reasons where demand is affected. If the predictions are towards the positive side the demand will rise. Whereas negative predictions will decrease the demand of goods.

4.10 Demand Function

Demand function means the functional relationship between demand and the factors affecting demands. When a commodity is demanded it is a result, when all factors which are affecting come into existence. All the factors which affects demand are put together is known as demand function.

$$DX = f(Px, P_R, Pc, Y, T, P, C, F, FT)$$

Where in..

DX	=	Demand Function
F	=	function of
Px	=	Price of a commodity
P_R	=	Price of the related commodity
Pc	=	Price of the complementary goods
Y	=	Income of the consumer
T	=	Change in Taste
P	=	Numbers if consumers
C	=	Climate and season
F	=	Future expectation
FT	=	Future trends

4.11 Variations in Demand

The change in demand or variations in demand means change in demand of a commodity. This happens due to change in price as well as other factors. Change in demand occurs due to various reasons such as change in the income of the consumers, change in price of related goods, taste, habits and preferences of the consumers etc. Let us understand with a diagram.

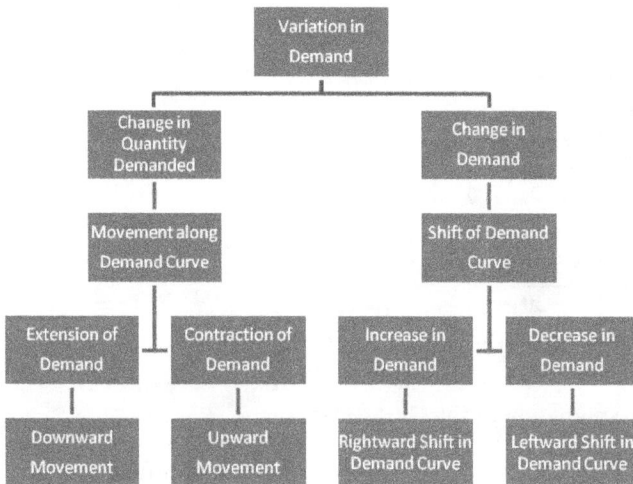

4.12 Change in Quantity Demanded

Change in quantity demanded means movement along a demand curve. It states that the consumers moves upwards or downwards along the same demand curve. It is caused by change in price alone. All the other determinants remaining constant if price rises, the consumer will decrease the demand and if price falls demand will increase. It is further classified into two parts.

A. Extension or Expansion of Demand

B. Contraction of Demand

A. Extension or Expansion of Demand

The expansion of demand occurs due to reduction in prices. For e.g. Commodity A is given at Rs. 10 / Kg. If the price of Commodity A decreases from Rs. 10 to Rs. 5 automatically the demand will increases from 1 Kg to 5 Kg. Such situation refers to expansion of demand. Let us understand with a schedule and graph.

Price	Quantity
15	5
10	10
5	20

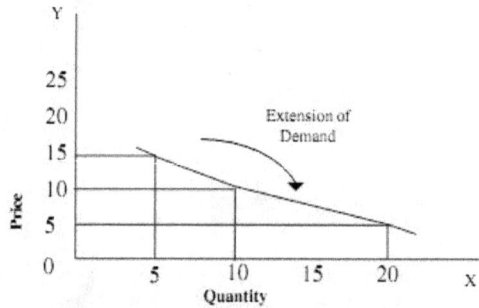

Explanation of the Curve / Graph

As per the observation of the graph it is clearly noticed that when the price of the commodity decreases the quantity demanded will rise. Therefore even when expansion is noticed, a downward curve is observed.

B. Contraction Demand

The contraction of demand occurs due to increase in prices. For e.g. Commodity B is given at Rs. 10 per Kg in the market. Now if the price of that commodity increases from Rs. 10 to Rs. 15 and demand goes down to 500 gm, this situation is referred as contraction of demand. Let us understand with a schedule and graph.

Price	Quantity
5	20
10	10
15	5

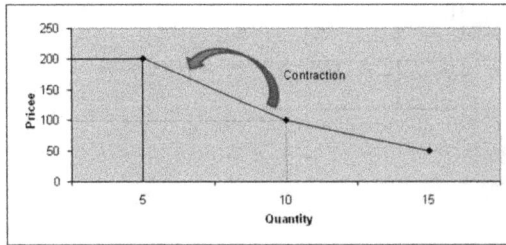

Explanation of the Curve / Graph

As per the observation it is clear that when price increases and quantity demanded decreases. Even after contraction of demand the curve is moving towards the upward side.

4.13 Change in Demand

Change in demand means that rightward shift or leftward shift of demand curve from its original. It states that consumers shift their demand towards the left or right of demand curve. It is caused by the factor other than price. It can be further classified into two parts :

A.   Increase in Demand

B.   Decrease in Demand

A. Increase in Demand

Increase in demand refers to a situation when there is more demand at the same price in such case it is referred to upward direction increase in demand. Let us understand with a schedule and graph.

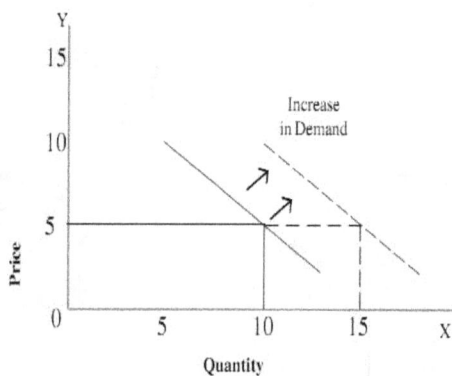

Price	Quantity
10	10
10	15

Explanation of the Curve / Graph

As per the observation from the above mentioned graph it is clear that price remain constant quantity demanded increase, The two lines in the graph clearly states that the consumer has shifted his demand towards rightward direction.

B. Decrease in Demand

Decrease in demand refers to either less quantity demanded at the same price or same quantity at that price. In such a case demand curve shifts towards the downwards direction. Let us understand with a schedule and graph.

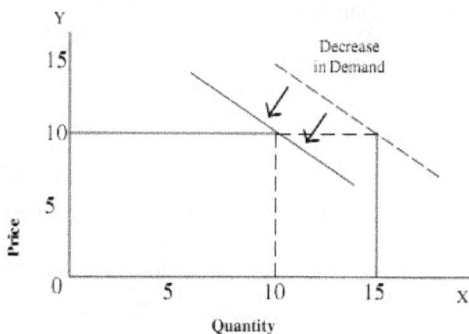

Price	Quantity
10	15
10	10

48

Explanation of the Curve / Graph

From the above graph it is observed that price being constant demand has a decreased line which shows that the consumer has shifted his demand towards direction or leftwards curve is observed.

4.14 Reasons for increase in Demand

- Due to increase in the income of the consumer.
- Due to increase in price of substitute goods.
- Due to increase in price of complementary goods.
- Positive change in taste, preference and habits.
- Positive change in climate and season

4.15 Reasons for decrease in Demand

- Due to decrease in the income of the consumer.
- Due to decrease in price of substitute goods.
- Due to decrease in price of complementary goods.
- Negative change in taste, preference and habits.
- Negative change in climate and season.

4.16 Distinguish between Quantity Demanded and Change in Demand

Basic	Quantity Demanded	Change in Demand
Price	It implies to a change in demand for any commodity due to change in its own price.	It implies to change in price of substitute goods, complementary goods, income of the consumers, taste, preferences and habits.

Movement of Demand Curve	It indicates movement along the demand curve.	It indicates shift in demand curve.
Price Fall and Demand	A fall in price of any commodity leads to an increase in quantity demanded.	A fall of other factors except the price of own commodity leads to increase in demand.
Price Rise and Demand	A rise in price will lead to decrease in quantity demanded.	Increase in other factors will lead to decrease in demand.
Curve	In this extension and contraction demand curve is observed	In this increase and decrease demand curve is observed.

4.17 Price Elasticity of Demand

Price elasticity of demand means change in quantity demanded of a commodity. In response to change in its price. In other words it measures the degree of change of demand in response to change in price. It indicates how consumers react to change in price. The greater the reaction greater will the elasticity lesser the reaction the smaller will be the elasticity.

Price elasticity of demand is a commonly called as elasticity of demand. This is because price is the most changeable factor which affects demand.

4.18 Definition of Elasticity of Demand

According to Alfred Marshall,

"Elasticity of demand may be defined as percentage (%) change in quantity demanded to percentage (%) change in price"

It is symbolically denoted as 'Ep'. It can be express by the following formulae,

$$Ep = \frac{\text{Percentage (\%) change in quantity demanded}}{\text{Percentage (\%) change in price}}$$

where symbolically,

$$\frac{\dfrac{\Delta Q \times 100}{Q}}{\dfrac{\Delta P \times 100}{P}}.$$

After simplification,

$$\frac{\Delta Q \times P}{\Delta P \times Q}$$

The above remain formulae can be understood as follows:

Δ = Delta / Change

P = Original price of a commodity

Q = Quantity demanded

ΔP = Delta in price

ΔQ = Delta in quantity demanded

4.19 Degree / Kind of Elasticity of Demand

Elasticity of demand differs from commodity to commodity and from individual to individual. A given change in price may lead to significant or small changes in quantity demanded. Economics have pointed out five degree / kind of elasticity of demand.

A.   Perfect Elastic Demand

B.   Perfect Inelastic Demand

C.   Inelastic Demand

D.   Elastic Demand

E.   Unitary Elasticity of Demand

The five degree / kind of elasticity of demand is as :

A. Perfect Elastic Demand

Demand is said to be perfect by using elastic when demand varies. They can be increase in demand or decrease in demand in observed but no change in price is notices. Price remains constant such situation can be denoted as, 'Ed' = ∞, which is known as infinite. Let us understand this with a schedule and a graph.

P	Q
10	5
10	10
10	15
10	20

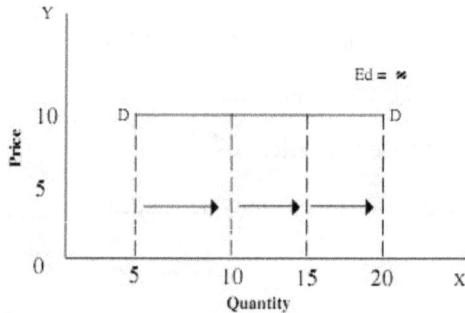

Explanation of the Curve / Graph

As per the observation it is clearly noticed that quantity keeps on increasing or decreasing but prices remains constant. In this graph a straight line is observed which states perfect elasticity of demand. It is denoted as Ed = ∞

B. Perfect Inelastic Demand

When quantity demanded does not change as a result of change in price of a commodity demanded. Such situation is referred as perfect inelastic demand. Here prices may increase or decrease but demand remains constant. Let us understand this with a schedule and a graph.

P	Q
5	20
10	20
15	20
20	20

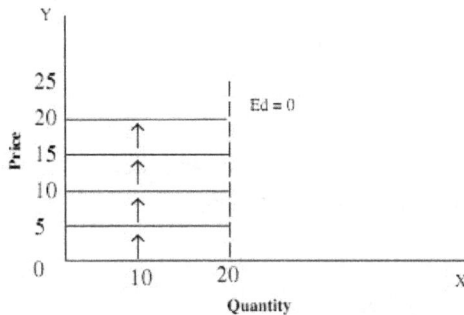

Explanation of the Curve / Graph

As per the observation form the above graph it is clearly noticed that there is a variations in price of commodities but the quantity demanded remains stable. No change in demand is seen. It can be denoted as Ed = 0.

C. Inelastic Demand

When a large change in price is observed in comparison to quantity demanded. This type of situation refers to inelastic demand. Here maximum change in price is observed with reference to its demand for its product. Let us understand this with a schedule and a graph.

P	Q
15	20
25	15

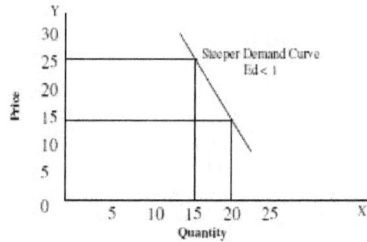

Explanation of the Curve / Graph

From the above graph it is clearly observed that more change in price is noticed with comparison to its quantity demanded. Price may vary an extent but demand defers in a small proportion. This is symbolically denoted as Ed < 1.

D. Elastic Demand

When there is a more change in quantity demand notice. The price changes at very small proportions. Here proportionate change in quantity is observed than price. Let us understand this with a schedule and a graph.

P	Q
20	30
25	15

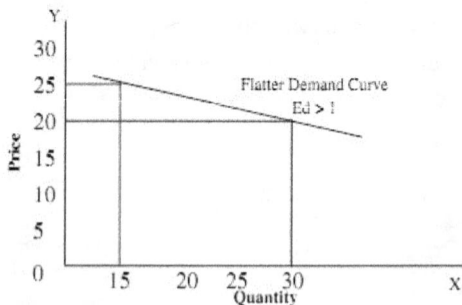

Explanation of the Curve / Graph

From the above graph it is clearly observed that more change in quantity is noticed with respect to its prices. This is symbolically denoted as Ed > 1.

E. Unitary elasticity of Demand

In this situation percentage (%) change in demand is equal to percentage (%) change in price. If elasticity of demand is equal to price, expenditure of a commodity will remain same even when price changes. Let us understand this with a schedule and a graph.

P	Q
20	15
10	30

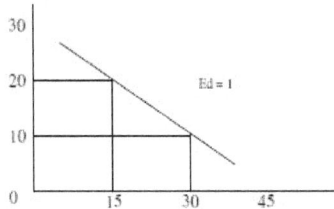

Explanation of the Curve / Graph

From the above graph it is clearly observed that proportionate change in quantity demand is equal to proportionate change in price, here Ed = 1.

4.20 Measurement of Price Elasticity of Demand

Price elasticity of demand expresses the responses of quantity demanded of a commodity to change in its price. Mainly there are two method of measuring price elasticity of demand.

A. Percentage Change Method

Percentage change method is also known as proportionate or mathematical method. According to this method percentage change method is measured by dividing the change in demand by change in price percentage (%) wise.

$$Ep = \frac{\text{percentage (\%) change in demand}}{\text{percentage (\%) change in price}}$$

where symbolically,

$$\frac{\dfrac{\Delta Q \times 100}{Q}}{\dfrac{\Delta P \times 100}{P}}$$

After simplification, $\dfrac{\Delta Q \times P}{\Delta P \times Q}$

Where,

Ep = Price elasticity of demand

P = Original price

Q = Original quantity demanded

ΔP = Change in price

ΔQ = Change in quantity demanded

B. Geometric or Point Method

Geometric or point method it is a method of measuring elasticity of demand given by Alfred Marshall. In this method a demand curve is drawn to measure it. Therefore it is known geometric or graphic or point method. i.e. ED. ED at any point is measured by dividing the length of lower segment of demand curve with the upper segment of demand curve at that point. The value of ED is unitary at mid point.

The steps to get elasticity of demand by geometric method are as follows:

i.   Draw x and y axis.

ii.   Draw a straight line, name it A and B. (Perfect negative line)

iii.   Divide AB into 5 equal point.

iv.   The middle point is P.

v.   The upper point ED, which is greater than 1, name it as P2.

vi.   The upper most point which is named as A, name it P1.

vii.   The lower most point which is named D = 0.

Let us understand with a schedule and a graph.

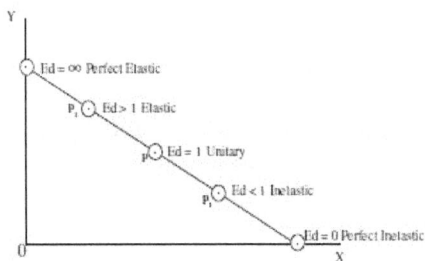

Explanation of the Curve / Graph

From the above graph it is clear that when Ed = ∞ perfect elastic demand occurs. Whereas when Ed>1 Elasticity in demand is found. When Ed=1 it shows a unitary elastic demand. Ed<1 describes the inelasticity in demand and when Ed=0 it denotes perfect inelastic.

4.21 Calculations of Price Elasticity of Demand

Example 1. Find out Ep from the following.

P	Q
10 (P)	20 (Q)
20	15
10 (ΔP)	5 (ΔQ)

$$Ep = \frac{\Delta Q \times P}{\Delta P \times Q} = \frac{5 \times 10}{10 \times 20}$$

$$\therefore Ep = 0.25$$

Therefore it is clear that price elasticity of demand is Ed < 1, i.e. 0.25. In such type of elasticity is said to be inelastic demand.

Example 2. Find out Ep from the following.

P	Q
100 (P)	1000 (Q)
102	900
2 (ΔP)	100 (ΔQ)

$$Ep = \frac{\Delta Q \times P}{\Delta P \times Q} = \frac{100 \times 100}{2 \times 1000}$$

$$\therefore Ep = 5$$

Therefore it is clear that price elasticity of demand is Ed > 1, i.e. 5. In such type of elasticity is said to be elastic demand.

Example 3. Find out Ep from the following.

P	Q
200 (P)	1000 (Q)
198	1100
-2 (ΔP)	100 (ΔQ)

$$Ep = \frac{\Delta Q \times P}{\Delta P \times Q} = \frac{100 \times 200}{-2 \times 1000}$$

$$\therefore Ep = -10$$

Therefore it is clear that price elasticity of demand is Ed < 1, i.e. -10. In such type of elasticity is said to be inelastic demand.

Example 4. The price of commodity has increased by 20% as a result demand declined by 20 unit to 15 unit, calculate Ep.

$$Ep = \frac{\Delta Q / Q1 \times 100}{Q1}$$

$$Ep = \frac{5 \times 100}{20}$$

$\therefore$ **Ep** = 1.25

Therefore it is clear that price elasticity of demand is Ed > 1, i.e. 1.25. In such type of elasticity is said to be elastic demand.

4.22 Relationship between Perfect Elasticity Demand and Total Expenditure Method

Prof Alfred Marshall suggest that,

"Change in total expenditure before and after the change in price of a commodity is studied."

There are three possibility that can survive:

- When ED is greater than 1, it is said to be demand is elastic. Here when the total expenditure increase with fall in price and total expenditure decreases with rise in price. There is an inverse relationship in this possibility.

- When elasticity of demand is less than 1, demand is inelastic. This happens when total expenditure remains same even when change in price occurs. Price may rise or fall but total expenditure (TE) remain same.

- When Perfect Elasticity is equal to units, i.e. ED = 1. Here its unitary elasticity. This happens when total expenditure (TE) decreases with fall in price and TE increases with rise in price. There is a positive relationship observed

4.23   Factors affecting Elasticity of Demand

Elasticity of demand for a commodity is influenced by numbers of factors some are as follows:

1.   Availability of Substitute Goods
2.   Postponement of Consumption
3.   Nature of Commodity
4.   Use of a Commodity
5.   Income of the Consumer
6.   Proportion of Expenditure
7.   Price Level

Let us understand in detail.

1.   Availability of Substitute Goods

One of the most important determinants of ED is availability of close substitute. The demand for commodities having large number of substitute goods will be more elastic. For e.g. Tea and Coffee are the substitute goods for each other whereas salt has no substitute. Therefore, inelastic it has demand.

2. Postponement of Consumption

The commodity whose consumption can be postponed will have elastic demand. Whereas those commodities whose consumption cannot be delayed will be inelastic in degree. For e.g. Price of a Car rises, its consumption can be delayed but use of medicines cannot be postponed.

3. Nature of Commodity

Commodities are broadly divided into two groups: Necessity and Luxuries. Necessities have high inelastic demand while luxuries have high ED. For e.g. Medicines are necessaries goods where as car is said to be luxuries product.

4. Use of a Commodity

If a commodity has many alternative uses demand will be elastic where as only limited use result into inelastic demand. For e.g. Milk have various alternative uses. Therefore it has elastic demand whereas medicine for special purpose has limited use. Therefore it has inelastic demand.

5. Income of the Consumer

Elasticity of demand will be less in case of consumers whose income is low as he may have limited funds to spend whereas more the income results into elastic demand as more money to spend in the market.

6. Proportion of Expenditure

Elasticity will be inelastic with regards to those goods on which consumer spend a very small friction of his total expenditure. For e.g. Salt, Matchbox etc on the other has elasticity will be elastic with regards to those goods on which a consumer spends more of his total expenditure.

7. Price Level

Price level of commodity the demand for goods having high price will be inelastic in demand where as the demand for goods having low price will be elastic. Higher the price quantity demanded will be low and lower the price quantity demand will be high.

4.24   Question Bank

1. Explain the concept of demand.
2. Define demand.
3. Justify Law of Demand with schedule and graph.
4. What is market demand?
5. Discuss the determinants of demand.
6. Explain demand function.
7. What is variation in demand?
8. Explain with graph change in quantity demanded.
9. Put in your own words what is change in demand with the help of graphs.
10. Explain contraction of demand.
11. What is extension of demand?
12. What do you mean by increase and decrease in demand?
13. State the reasons for increase and decrease in demand.
14. Explain the concept of price elasticity of demand.
15. Discuss the degrees of price elasticity of demand.
16. How will you measure price elasticity of demand?
17. Discuss geometric method of price elasticity of demand.
18. Discuss the relationship between perfect elasticity and total expenditure method.
19. Explain factors determining elasticity of demand.
20. A consumer buys 40 units of a product at Rs. 5/- per unit given that Ep = (-2), how much of the commodity will he buy if price falls to Rs. 4/- per unit?   (Ans: 56)
21. A consumer buys 80 units of a commodity at Rs 4/-unit. As price fall he buys 100 units of the commodity. If Ep= (-1) the find the new price of the commodity.   (Ans: Rs. 3/unit)

64

Chapter - 5

Production Function

In this Chapter you will clear your concepts about…..

➤ *Concept of Production Function*

➤ *An Isoquant*

➤ *Types of Product*

  ❖ *Total Product (TP)*

  ❖ *Average Product (AP)*

  ❖ *Marginal Product (MP)*

➤ *Relationship between Total Product (TP), Average Product (AP) and Marginal Product (MP)*

➤ *Calculations of Average Product (AP) and Marginal Product (MP) from Total*

Chapter - 5

Production Function

5.1 Introduction

There is a direct relationship between the amount of input, i.e. land, labour, capital, raw material, entrepreneur etc., and the amount of output, i.e. finished commodity. The functional relationship between the physical input and physical output of a firm is an essential part of any of the Production Company or factory. It is important for any entrepreneur to understand how a certain amount of input will result into production of certain amount of output in form of a commodity.

5.2 Concept of Production Function

In a very simple way to understand this concept of production function, the relationship between input and output is observed and symbolically denoted as 'Q'. It is nearly transformation of input into output. A technological relationship showing maximum output that can be produced from various combinations of input is known as production function. Factors of production can be termed as input whereas the fruit of their productive activity can be termed as output.

According to Waston, "Production function is the relation between a firm's production (output) and material factor of production (input). "

Therefore, $Q = f(f_1, f_2, f_3 \ldots \ldots f_n)$

Where, Q = Production function

f = factors of production

Let us understand this concept with an example. A shoe manufacturing company has one worker, one machine and 10 Kgs of raw material. This can produce 10 pair of shoes. Whereas two workers, two machines and 20 Kgs of raw material. This can produce 20 pair of shoes. Then this is said to be an ideal position where maximum output from input can be observed.

5.3   An Isoquant

An Isoquant is very much similar to indifference curve and map. An indifference curve is a schedule of various combinations of commodities which may be equally satisfactory to the consumer's concern. In the similar way and Isoquant is set of all possible combinations of two input that can yield maximum possible level of output. Let us understand with a graph.

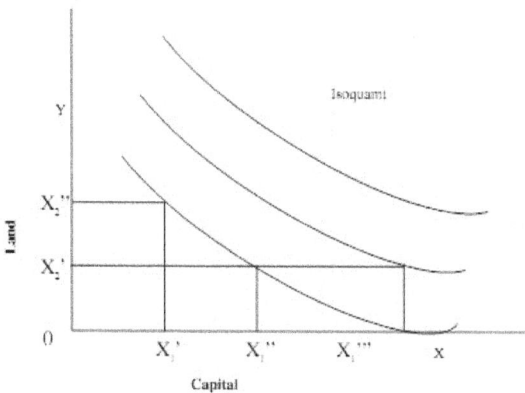

Explanation of the Curve / Graph

Now when one input is increased to the first factor of production (input) the output will tend to increase. Slowly and steadily when output increases with additional input reaches the highest Isoquant. When marginal products are positive, the same level of output can be produced by using high technologies and lesser stress. The slope of Isoquant will always be in downward position.

5.4   Types of Product

Product or output refers to the volume of goods produced by a firm during a specific period of time. The volume of goods produced can be divided into three types/kinds. They are as follows:

1. Total Product (TP)

2. Average Product (AP)

3. Marginal Product (MP)

Let us understand the above types of product in detail.

A. Total Product (TP)

Total product refers to the total volume of goods produced during a period of time. This can be raised only by increasing the quantity of factors employed in production. Let us understand with a schedule and a graph.

Labour (f)	TP
1	10
2	20
3	30
4	40
5	50

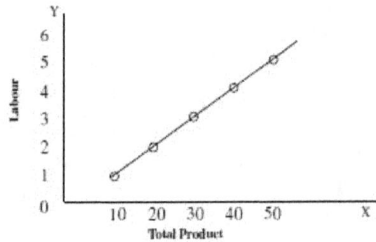

Explanation of the Curve / Graph

From the above graph it is clear that the labourers who work during a time period gives an output which in total is termed as Total Product (TP) of the firm. This increases as the input increases.

B. Average Product (AP)

Average product can be calculated by dividing total product by the number of input given. The formula for calculation of average product is TP/X_1. Here TP = total product and X_1 is input. It is also known as the per unit product for a variable factor. Let us understand with a schedule and a graph.

Labour (f)	TP	AP
1	30	30
2	80	40
3	120	40
4	150	37.5
5	170	34

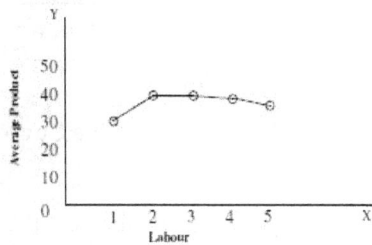

Explanation of the Curve / Graph

From the above graph it is clear that the average product at the beginning point keeps on increasing at an increasing rate. As input increases, slowly and steadily it becomes constant and then starts falling at a diminishing rate. It is observed that Average product starts declining when total product and X_1 is at its highest.

C. Marginal Product (MP)

The rate at which total product increases is known as marginal product. We can define marginal product as the additional unit to the total product resulting from increasing quantity from the variable factor. The formula for finding Marginal Product MP is $MP = TP(n) - TP(n-1)$. Let us understand with a schedule and a graph.

Labour (f)	TP	MP
1	30	-
2	80	50
3	120	40
4	150	30
5	170	20

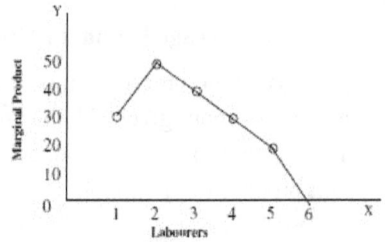

Explanation of the Curve / Graph

From the above graph it is clear that the marginal product rises at the beginning but ultimately it begins to fall and becomes zero and turns into negative also. This shows that when total product is maximum, marginal product will be zero.

5.5 Relationship between Total Product (TP), Average Product (AP) and Marginal Product (MP)

The Total Product (TP), Average Product (AP) and Marginal Product (MP) are interdependent to each other. If Total Product (TP) is affected, the other two will have a change in it. Their relationship can be mentioned as follows:

1. When Total Product (TP) increases, Average Product (AP) and Marginal Product (MP) will also increase.
2. When Total Product (TP) is at its highest, Average Product (AP) will start declining and Marginal Product (MP) will turn into zero.

3. When Total Product (TP) starts declining, Average Product (AP) will start falling at a diminishing rate and Marginal Product (MP) will go towards negative.

5.6 Calculations of Average Product (AP) and Marginal Product (MP) from Total Product(TP)

Ex-1 Calculations of Average Product (AP) and Marginal Product (MP) from the given table:

Factor	1	2	3	4	5	6	7	8	9	10
TP	80	170	270	368	430	480	504	504	495	480

Ans -1

Factor	TP	AP	MP
1	80	80	80
2	170	85	90
3	270	90	100
4	368	92	98
5	430	86	72
6	480	80	50
7	504	72	24
8	504	63	0
9	495	55	-9
10	480	48	-15

Formulae used to calculate the above table:

1. AP = TP / Input (f)
2. MP = TP(n)- TP(n-1)

Ex-2 Complete the following table:

Factor	TP	AP	MP
1	20	?	?
2	45	?	?
3	?	?	27
4	?	25	?
5	100	?	?
6	?	15	?
7	?	?	-8
8	?	8	?

Ans-2

Factor	TP	AP	MP
1	20	20	20
2	45	22.5	25
3	72	24	27
4	100	25	28
5	100	20	0
6	90	15	-10
7	82	11.71	-8
8	64	8	-18

Formulae used to calculate the above table:

1. AP = TP / Input (f)
2. TP = AP * Factor
3. TP = TP(n) + MP
4. MP = TP(n)- TP(n-1)

5.7 Question Bank

1. Explain the concept of production function.

2. What is an Isoquant?

3. Explain total product with the help of a graph.

4. Explain average product with the help of a graph.

5. Explain marginal product with the help of a graph.

6. Discuss the relationship of TP, AP and MP in a single graph.

7. Calculate TP and AP from the following table.

X	1	2	3	4	5	6	7
MP	24	22	16	12	8	0	-8

8. Calculate TP and MP from the following table.

X	1	2	3	4	5	6
AP	2	3	4	4.25	4	3.50

9. Calculate MP and AP from the following table.

X	0	1	2	3	4	5
TP	0	15	35	50	40	48

Chapter - 6

Returns to a Factor and Returns to a Scale

In this Chapter you will clear your concepts about.....

➢ *Concept of Returns to a Factor / Law of Variable Proportion*

➢ *Law of Variable Proportion / Returns to a Factor*

➢ *Statement of the Law of Variable Proportion*

➢ *Stages of Law of Variable Proportion*

➢ *Returns to a Scale*

➢ *Statement of the Returns to a Scale*

➢ *Stages of Law of Returns to a Scale*

➢ *Differentiation between Returns to a Factor and Returns to a Scale*

Chapter - 6

Returns to a Factor and Returns to a Scale

6.1   Introduction

The supply of a commodity always depends upon its cost of production which in turn upon :-

(a) Physical relationship between input and output.

(b) Pricing factor

The physical relationship between factors and output plays an important role in determining cost of production. This directly refers to

i.   Returns to a Factor

ii.   Returns to a Scale

6.2   Concept of Returns to a Factor / Law of Variable Proportion

When the quantity of one variable factor is increases keeping the other factors constant which results into increase in output is called Returns to a Factor. More precisely known as Returns to a Variable Factor. The returns to a factor may be expressed in terms of Total Product (TP), Average Product (AP) and Marginal Product (MP).

6.3   Law of Variable Proportion / Returns to a Factor

Law of Variable Proportion occupies an important place in economic theories. This examines the production function of one variable factor keeping the quantities of other factors fixed. In other words, it refers to input-output relationship.

6.4   Statement of the Law of Variable Proportion

"An increase in the quantity of one input keeping other inputs fixed, the total product increases at increasing rate in the beginning and then increases at decreasing rate after a level, and then ultimately falls"

6.5   Stages of Law of Variable Proportion

The behavior of Total Product (TP), Average Product (AP) and Marginal Product (MP) of the variable factor results into an increase is generally divided into three stages.

i.   Stage of Increasing Returns

ii.   Stage of Diminishing Returns

iii.   Stage of Negative returns

Lets us understand in detail.

Stage No. 1: Stage of Increasing Returns

In this stage Total Product (TP) to a point increases at an increasing rate at the starting point. Several causes affect this increase. The main reasons that affect the rise can be listed as follows:

a. High efficiency of laborers

b. Full utilization of resources

c. High individual capacity

d. Use of high technologies

e. Specialization of factors indulged in it.

Stage No. 2: Stage of Decreasing Returns

In this stage Total Product (TP) continues to increase at a diminishing ratio until it reaches to its maximum point. Total Product (TP) increases at a lower rate but remains positive at this stage. A continuous fall is noticed. The main reasons that affect this can be listed as follows:

    a. Less efficiency of laborers

    b. Less utilization of resources

    c. Divided individual capacity

    d. Less cooperation

Stage No. 3: Stage of Negative Returns

In this stage Total Product (TP) declines and the curve slopes downwards towards negative direction. The main reasons that affect this can be listed as follows:

    a.   Dull efficiency of laborers

    b.   Negligible utilization of resources

    c.   Negligible individual capacity

    d.   No cooperation

    e.   Obstructive behavior

Let us understand this Law with the help of a schedule and a graph.

Input	Output
1	1
2	2
3	3
4	5
5	7
6	8
7	7
8	6
9	5
10	0
11	-1

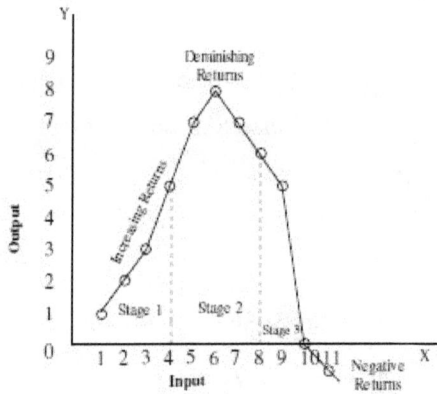

Explanation of the Curve / Graph

The above graph shows that there is an increase at an increasing rate at the starting point. This is the Stage of Increasing Returns. Then at a level starts declining at a diminishing rate. This is the Stage of Diminishing Returns and at the later part starts falling at an increasing rate and turns towards negative slope facing downwards. This is the Stage of Negative Returns. Thus the shape of the curve will always be inverse 'U' shape.

6.6 Assumption of the Law

The assumption of the Law of Variable Proportion can be stated as follows:

1. The state of technology is assumed to be given and unchanged.

2. When one input is increases, other outputs should remain constant.

3. This is all related with short period or short run

6.7 Returns to a Scale

In Law of Variable Proportion, we studied as how a variable of a production is increased keeping other factors fixed leads to raise in Total Product (TP) at an increasing rate in the beginning. Later diminishing the returns and ultimately towards negative. This is all related with short period or short run. Some factors are fixed, only one changes in short run. But when it is discussed with long run, every factor has right to change. It varies as per the demand of production.

6.8 Statement of the Returns to a Scale

"The Returns to a Scale refers to the change in output as all factors of production that is inputs changes at the same proportion in long run". The question arises is at what rate the output will increase when all inputs are varying at same proportion? There can be three possibilities. The increase in output may be more than, equal to or less than it's input. The Law of Returns to a Scale with its three stages can be understood with an example.

Scales of Production				Total Production
1 Machine	+	2 Labourers	=	100 units
2 Machines	+	4 Labourers	=	250 units
4 Machines	+	8 Labourers	=	600 units
⇩				
Increasing Returns to a Scale (IRS)				
Scales of Production				Total Production
8 Machines	+	16 Labourers	=	1600 units
16 Machines	+	32 Labourers	=	3200 units
⇩				
Constant Returns to a Scale (CRS)				
Scales of Production				Total Production
32 Machines	+	64 Labourers	=	4000 units
64 Machines	+	128 Labourers	=	7000 units
⇩				
Diminishing Returns to a Scale (DRS)				

6.9   Stages of Law of Returns to a Scale

The Law of Returns of a Scale is mainly divided into three stages as discussed in the above example. These stages can be named as:

i.   Increasing Returns to a Scale (IRS)

ii.   Constant Returns to a Scale (CRS)

iii.   Diminishing Returns to a Scale (DRS)

Lets us understand in detail.

Stage No. 1: Increasing Returns to a Scale (IRS)

An increasing return to a scale is observed when all the variable factors that is machines, workers, capital, etc. are increased at the same proportion resulting into increases in output comparatively. When the input is increased the output is more than expected.

Stage No. 2: Constant Returns to a Scale (CRS)

In this stage the input is increased in the same proportion and the output gained is also in the same proportion. The ratio of increase in input as well as output remains constant proportionately.

Stage No. 3: Diminishing Returns to a Scale (DRS)

In the diminishing returns to a scale, the output diminishes or decreases at an increasing rate due to several reasons such as:

      a. Dull efficiency of laborers

      b. Negligible utilization of resources

      c. Negligible individual capacity

      d. No cooperation

      e. Obstructive behavior

Let us understand this Law with the help of a schedule and a graph.

Input	Output
1	2
2	5
3	5
4	5
5	5
6	1

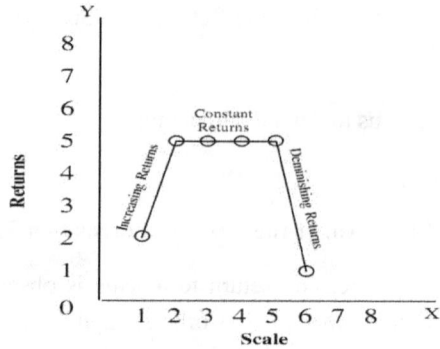

Explanation of the Curve / Graph

The above graph it is clear that Point A & B shows the Increasing Returns to a Scale (IRS). Whereas Point B & C shows Constant Returns to a Scale (CRS) and Point C & D shows Diminishing Returns to a Scale (DRS).When all inputs are variable at the same proportion, comparatively output is distinguished from each other, i.e. IRS, CRS and DRS. This is said to be Law of Returns to a Scale. Thus the shape of the curve will always be inverse 'U' shape.

6.10   Assumption of the Law

The assumption of the Law of Returns to a Scale can be stated as follows:

1. The state of technology is assumed to be changed and new techniques are introduced.

2. When all inputs are variable at the same proportion, comparatively output is distinguished from each other.

3. This is all related with long period or long run.

6.11 Differentiation between Returns to a Factor and Returns to a Scale

Sr. No.	Aspects	Returns to a Factor	Returns to a Scale
1.	Time span	It is operated in short run or short term.	It is operated in long run or long term.
2.	Change in variable	Only one input factor changes, keeping other factors constant.	When all inputs are variable at the same proportion.
3.	Factor Ratio	There is a change in factor ratio.	There is no change in factor ratio.
4.	Volume	A change in Scales of volume of production is not observed.	A change in Scales of volume of production is observed.
5.	Technology	The technology due to short run can be assumed to be constant or unchanged.	In long run, possibilities to new technologies can be introduced.

6.12 Question Bank

1. State the concept of Returns to a Factor.

2. Explain the Law of Variable Proportion with its stages and diagram.

3. Discuss Returns to a scale with an example and a graph.

4. Differentiate Returns to a factor and Returns to a scale.

Chapter - 7

Costs

In this Chapter you will clear your concepts about…..

- ➢ *Time Element of Cost*
    - ❖ *Short Run / Short Period*
    - ❖ *Long Run / Long Period*
- ➢ *Types of Cost*
    - ❖ *Total Fixed Cost (T.F.C.)*
    - ❖ *Total Cost (T.C.)*
    - ❖ *Average Fixed Cost (A.F.C.)*
    - ❖ *Average Variable Cost (A.V.C.)*
    - ❖ *Average Cost (A.C.)*
    - ❖ *Marginal Cost (M.C.)*
- ➢ *Formulae to calculate Costs*
- ➢ *Calculations of the Costs Using Formulae*

Chapter - 7

Costs

7.1 Introduction

The term cost is very familiar to us. It is directly related to cost of production. Cost of production means total expenditure on a product to make it possible for sales. It refers to the expenses incurred on production of a commodity.

The force of demand and supply determines the price of a commodity in a free competitive market. The demand for a commodity is influenced by its utility and consumer preference. Similarly, supply of commodity is influenced by its cost of production. Therefore, it is essential to understand this concept.

7.2 Time Element of Cost

Time element plays an essential role in the analysis of cost of production. In economics, there are basically two kinds of time period. i.e. short run and long run. Let us understand these two kinds of time period in detail.

A. Short Run / Short Period

During this period, production is the basic point to be kept in mind. Production is the base for the change that happens during this time period. Mainly there are two types of cost. i.e. fixed cost and variable cost. Fixed cost the cost incurred on land, factory, building, heavy capital equipments, etc. which cannot be changed in short period. Whereas, variable cost the cost incurred on electricity consumption, fuel, wages to labourers, raw material expenses etc. It varies with the reference to the production or the output.

B. Long Run / Long Period

In long run or the long period, all the factors of production whether it is fixed or variable have possibilities to change. Long period is defined as the period which is long enough for all the inputs to be changed. Any changes in the concerned to the input is entertained and whole heartedly welcomed and accepted.

Let us discuss Time Period Element along with the concept of Costs with the help of a flow chart.

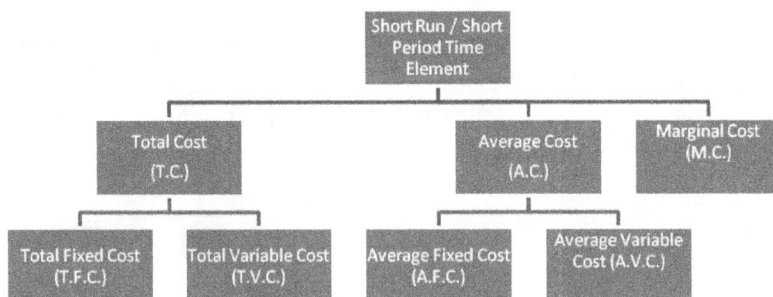

7.3 Types of Cost

As per the short run time element there are seven different types of Costs. Let us understand every cost along with the short run time element.

1. Total Fixed Cost (T.F.C.)

Total Fixed Cost (T.F.C.) remains constant at all levels of output. According to Murad, "Total Fixed Cost (T.F.C.) does not change with the change in the quantity of output." Therefore, Total Fixed Cost (T.F.C.) is also termed as Period Cost. For example, License fees, rent of office, insurance of building / factory, machines etc. Total Fixed Cost (T.F.C.) remains constant even if the output is zero. Total Fixed Cost (T.F.C.) is to be incurred at any situation or circumstances. It can be also termed as Committed Expense Cost. Let us understand this with a schedule and a graph.

Quantity	T.F.C
10	5
10	10

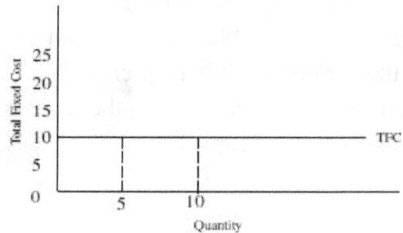

Explanation of the Curve / Graph

From the above graph it is clear that let the output be zero or more than that Total Fixed Cost (T.F.C.) remains stable or constant. These costs cannot be omitted. Therefore, Total Fixed Cost (T.F.C.) is one of the expenses which is compulsory to be attended.

2. Total Variable Cost (T.V.C.)

Total Variable Cost (T.V.C.) is cost which varies as per its name. This cost changes with the increase and decrease of output or the production. It changes with the change in the level of output or the production. When output is zero, it will be zero and vice versa. It is also termed as Direct Cost. For instance, cost incurred on raw material, wages of casual workers, maintenance of machinery etc.

According to Dooley, "Total Variable Cost (T.V.C.) is one which varies as the level of output varies." There are two phases of Total Variable Cost (T.V.C.): In the first phase, Total Variable Cost (T.V.C.) rises at decreasing rate. It means every new unit of output produced involves a lower cost therefore, the increase in efficiency of variable is observed. In the second phase, Total

88

Variable Cost (T.V.C.) rises at an increasing rate. It means every new output involves high cost as compared to previous ones. This is due to fall of efficiency of variable inputs. Let us understand this with a schedule and a graph.

Quantity	T.V.C
5	5
10	10
15	15
20	20

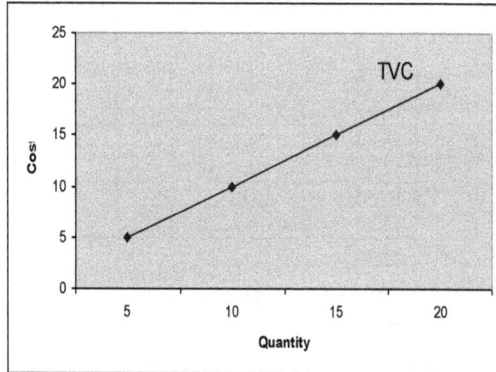

Explanation of the Curve / Graph

From the above graph it is clear that as quantity or the output increases, Total Variable Cost (T.V.C.) will increase and as and when the quantity or the output decreases, Total Variable Cost (T.V.C.) will fall down.

3. Total Cost (T.C.)

Total Cost (T.C.) is the sum of fixed cost and variable cost or producing any amount of output.

According to Dooley, "Total Cost (T. C.) of production is the sum of all expenses incurred in producing a given volume of output." Total Cost (T. C.) is the sum of Total Fixed Cost (T.F.C.) and Total Variable Cost (T.V.C.). Since Total Fixed Cost (T.F.C.) is constant at all levels of output, Total Cost (T. C.) will always exceed Total Variable Cost (T.V.C.) by the amount of Total Fixed Cost (T.F.C.). To get a Total Cost (T. C.), Total Fixed Cost (T.F.C.) and Total Variable Cost (T.V.C.) are very essential. Let us understand this with a schedule and a graph.

Quantity	T.F.C	T.V.C	T.C.
0	20	0	20
1	20	10	30
2	20	18	38
3	20	24	44
4	20	28	48

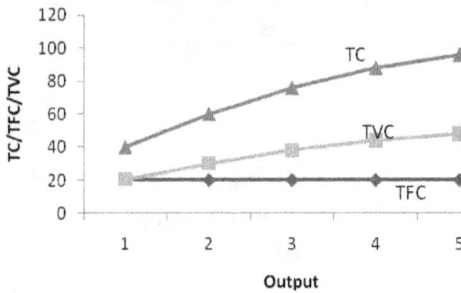

Explanation of the Curve / Graph

From the above graph it is clear that Total Cost (T.C.) is the vertical sum of Total Fixed Cost (T.F.C.) and Total Variable Cost (T.V.C.).

4. Average Fixed Cost (A.F.C.)

Average Fixed Cost (A.F.C.) is the Total Fixed Cost (T.F.C.) divided by the numbers of unit produced, i.e. output or the quantity. By dividing Total Fixed Cost (T.F.C.) by the total output, we get Average Fixed Cost (A.F.C.).

Formula to find out:

Average Fixed Cost (A.F.C.) = Total Fixed Cost (T.F.C.)

Total Output

As output increases, Average Fixed Cost (A.F.C.) falls as Total Fixed Cost (T.F.C.) is constant. Let us understand this with a schedule and a graph.

Quantity	T.F.C	A.F.C
0	20	0
1	20	20
2	20	10
3	20	6.66
4	20	5
5	20	4
6	20	3.33

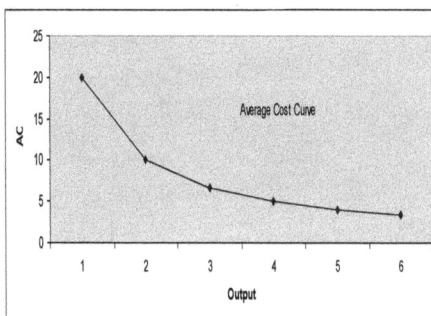

Explanation of the Curve / Graph

From the above graph it is clear that with the increase Total Fixed Cost (T.F.C.) Average Fixed Cost (T.F.C.) declines.

5. Average Variable Cost (A.V.C.)

Average Variable Cost (A.V.C.) can be observed by dividing the Total Variable Cost (T.V.C.) by the quantity. Average Variable Cost (A.V.C.) is variable cost per unit. It generally falls as output increases from zero to normal output. In other words, per unit of variable cost of production is termed as Average Variable Cost (A.V.C.).

91

Formula to find out:

Average Variable Cost (A.V.C.) =

Total Variable Cost (T.V.C.)

Total Output

Let us understand this with a schedule and a graph.

Quantity	T.V.C	A.V.C
0	0	0
1	18	18
2	30	15
3	40	13.33
4	52	13
5	65	13
6	82	13.66
7	106	15.14
8	140	17.50

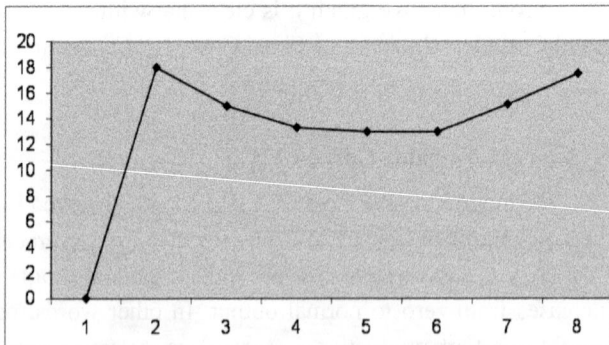

Explanation of the Curve / Graph

From the above graph it is clear that as output rises, Average Variable Cost (A.V.C.) initially falls down, reaches at a minimum level and then begins to rise. Therefore, Average Variable Cost (A.V.C.) curve is 'U' shaped due to Law of Diminishing Returns.

6. Average Cost (A.C.)

Average Cost (A.C.) is obtained by dividing the total cost by the quantity produced. In the other words, sum of Average Fixed Cost (A.F.C.) and Average Variable Cost (A.V.C.) is equal to Average Cost (A.C.). It is also known as Per Unit Cost.

Formula to find out:

$$\text{Average Cost (A.C.)} = \frac{\text{Total Cost (T.C.)}}{\text{Total Output}}$$

Diagrammatically, the summation of Average Fixed Cost (A.F.C.) and Average Variable Cost (A.V.C.) gives Average Cost (A.C.) curve. This curve is also 'U' shaped. As the Average Cost (A.C.) is the summation of Average Fixed Cost (A.F.C.) and Average Variable Cost (A.V.C.), Average Cost (A.C.) curve and Average Variable Cost (A.V.C.) curve will never intersect each other as well as Average Cost (A.C.) curve will always lie on the top of Average Variable Cost (A.V.C.) curve. Let us understand this with a schedule and a graph.

Quantity	A.F.C	A.V.C	A.C.
1	0	0	0
2	20	18	38
3	10	15	25
4	6.66	13.33	19.99
5	5	13	18
6	4	13	17
7	3.33	13.66	16.99

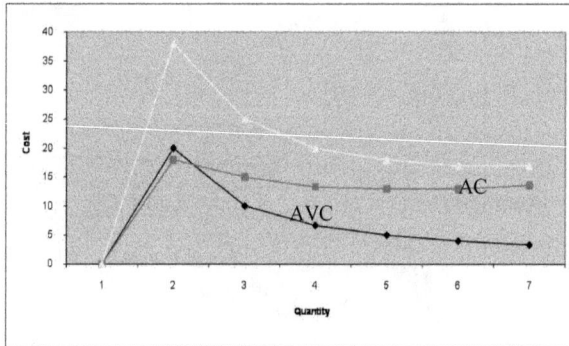

Explanation of the Curve / Graph

From the above graph it is clear that as the shape of Average Cost (A.C.) curve depends upon the shape of Average Fixed Cost (A.F.C.) curve and Average Variable Cost (A.V.C.) curve, it tends to slope downwards. Both Average Fixed Cost (A.F.C.) curve and Average Variable Cost (A.V.C.) curve are sloping downwards, Average Cost (A.C.) curve tends to be in the same position. Therefore, it is 'U' shaped.

7. Marginal Cost (M.C.)

Marginal Cost (M.C.) is the additional cost of producing additional units of output or the quantity. According to Ferguson, "Marginal Cost (M.C.) is the addition to total cost due to addition of one more unit."

Formula to find out:

$$\text{Marginal Cost (M.C.)} = \text{Total Cost (T.C.)}_n - \text{Total Cost (T.C.)}_{n-1}$$

Let us understand this with a schedule and a graph.

Quantity	T.C	M.C.
0	100	-
1	125	25
2	145	20
3	160	15
4	180	20
5	206	26
6	236	30
7	273	37

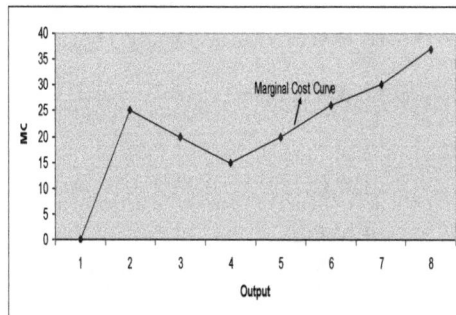

Explanation of the Curve / Graph

From the above graph it is clear that it is worth pointing that Marginal Cost (M.C.) is independent of the Fixed Costs. Since fixed costs do not change with the output, there will be no Marginal Fixed Cost (M.F.C.). As an assumption, output is increased only in short run period.

7.4 Formulae to calculate Costs

The formulae to find out different types of Costs are as follows:

1. T.C. $=$ T.F.C + T.V.C
2. T.C. $=$ A.C. X Q (Quantity or the output)
3. T.F.C. $=$ T.C. – T.V.C.
4. T.F.C. $=$ AFC X Q
5. T.V.C $=$ T.C. – T.F.C.
6. T.V.C. $=$ A.V.C. X Q
7. T.V.C. $=$ T.V.C. + M.C. (when given in the sum)
8. A.F.C. $=$ T.F.C. / Q
9. A.F.C. $=$ A.C. – A.V.C.
10. A.V.C. $=$ T.V.C. / Q
11. A.V.C. $=$ A.C. – A.F.C.
12. A.C. $=$ T.C. / Q
13. A.C. $=$ A.F.C. + A.V.C.
14. M.C. $=$ $T.C._n - T.C._{n-1}$
15. M.C. $=$ $T.V.C._n - T.V.C._{n-1}$
16. M.C. $=$ $\Delta T.V.C. / \Delta Q$

7.5   Calculations of the Costs Using Formulae

Sum-1.   Calculate T.V.C., A.F.C., A.V.C., A.F.C., A.C., and M.C. when Quantity, T.C. and T.F.C. are given.

Quantity	T.C.	T.F.C.	T.V.C.	A.F.C.	A.V.C.	A.C.	M.C.
FOR-MULA	(GIVEN IN THE SUM)	(GIVEN IN THE SUM)	T.C. - T.F.C	T.F.C. / Q	T.V.C. / Q	A.F.C + A.V.C	T.C.n- T.C. n-1
0	40	40	0	0	0	0	0
1	70	40	30	40	30	70	30
2	95	40	55	20	27.5	47.5	25
3	130	40	90	13.33	30	43.33	35
4	170	40	130	10	32.5	42.5	40
5	220	40	180	8	36	44	50

Sum-2.   Calculate T.V.C., A.F.C., A.V.C., A.F.C., A.C., and M.C. when Quantity, T.C. and T.F.C. are given.

Quantity	T.C.	T.F.C.	T.V.C.	A.F.C.	A.V.C.	A.C.	M.C.
FORMULAE	(GIVEN IN THE SUM)	(GIVEN IN THE SUM)	T.C. - T.F.C	T.F.C. / Q	T.V.C. / Q	A.F.C + A.V.C	T.C.n- T.C. n-1
0	60	60	0	0	0	0	0
1	78	60	18	60	18	78	18
2	90	60	30	30	15	45	12
3	102	60	42	20	14	34	12
4	112	60	52	15	13	28	10
5	120	60	60	12	12	24	8

Sum-3. Calculate T.C., A.F.C., A.V.C., A.F.C., A.C., and M.C. when Quantity, T.F.C. and T.V.C. are given.

Quantity	T.C.	T.F.C.	T.V.C.	A.F.C.	A.V.C.	A.C.	M.C.
FORMULAE	T.F.C. + T.V.C	(GIVEN IN THE SUM)	(GIVEN IN THE SUM)	T.F.C. / Q	T.V.C. / Q	A.F.C + A.V.C	T.C.n- T.C. n-1
0	60	60	0	0	0	0	0
1	80	60	20	60	20	80	20
2	90	60	30	30	15	45	10
3	120	60	60	20	20	40	30

Sum-4. Calculate T.C., A.F.C., A.V.C., A.F.C., A.C., and M.C. when Quantity, T.F.C. and T.V.C. are given.

Quantity	T.C.	T.F.C.	T.V.C.	A.F.C.	A.V.C.	A.C.	M.C.
FORMULAE	T.F.C. + T.V.C	(GIVEN IN THE SUM)	(GIVEN IN THE SUM)	T.F.C. / Q	T.V.C. / Q	A.F.C + A.V.C	T.C.n- T.C. n-1
0	80	80	0	0	0	0	0
1	105	80	25	80	25	105	25
2	110	80	30	40	15	55	5
3	120	80	40	26.67	13.33	40	10
4	130	80	50	20	12.5	32.5	10
5	135	80	55	16	11	27	5
6	140	80	60	13.33	10	23.33	5
7	148	80	68	11.43	9.71	21.14	8
8	152	80	72	10	9	19	4

Sum-5. Calculate T.V.C., T.C., A.F.C., A.V.C., A.F.C., and A.C. when Quantity, T.F.C. and M.C. are given.

Quantity	T.C.	T.F.C.	T.V.C.	A.F.C.	A.V.C.	A.C.	M.C.
FORMULAE	T.F.C. + T.V.C	(GIVEN IN THE SUM)	PREVIOUS ANSWER OF T.V.C. + M.C.	T.F.C. /Q	T.V.C. / Q	A.F.C + A.V.C	(GIVEN IN THE SUM)
0	240	120	120	0	0	0	-
1	160	120	40	120	40	160	40
2	190	120	70	60	35	95	30
3	216	120	96	40	32	72	26

Sum-6. Calculate T.V.C., T.C., A.F.C., A.V.C., A.F.C., and A.C. when Quantity, T.F.C. and M.C. are given.

Quantity	T.C.	T.F.C.	T.V.C.	A.F.C.	A.V.C.	A.C.	M.C.
FORMULAE	T.F.C. + T.V.C	(GIVEN IN THE SUM)	PREVIOUS ANSWER OF T.V.C. + M.C.	T.F.C. /Q	T.V.C. / Q	A.F.C + A.V.C	(GIVEN IN THE SUM)
1	90	60	30	60	30	90	30
2	116	60	56	30	28	58	26
3	144	60	84	20	28	48	28
4	176	60	116	15	29	44	32

Sum-7. Calculate T.V.C., T.C., A.F.C., A.V.C., A.F.C., and A.C. when Quantity, T.F.C. and M.C. are given.

Quantity	T.C.	T.F.C.	T.V.C.	A.F.C.	A.V.C.	A.C.	M.C.
FORMULAE	T.F.C. + T.V.C	(GIVEN IN THE SUM)	PREVIOUS ANSWER OF T.V.C. + M.C.	T.F.C. / Q	T.V.C. / Q	A.F.C + A.V.C	(GIVEN IN THE SUM)
1	4000	2000	2000	2000	2000	4000	2000
2	5500	2000	3500	1000	1750	2750	1500
3	6700	2000	4700	666.67	1566.67	2233.33	1200
4	8200	2000	6200	500	1550	2050	1500
5	10200	2000	8200	400	1640	2040	2000
6	12900	2000	10900	333.33	1816.67	2150	2700
7	16400	2000	14400	285.71	2057.14	2342.86	3500

Sum-8. Complete the following table.

Quantity	T.C.	T.F.C.	T.V.C.	A.F.C.	A.V.C.	A.C.	M.C.
1	12	12	12	?	12	?	12
2	?	12	20	6	?	?	?
3	42	12	?	?	?	?	10
4	?	12	40	?	?	?	?

Answer-8.

Quantity	T.C.	T.F.C.	T.V.C.	A.F.C.	A.V.C.	A.C.	M.C.
FORMULAE	T.F.C. + T.V.C	(GIVEN IN THE SUM)	T.F.C. - T.C.	T.F.C. / Q	T.V.C. / Q	A.F.C + A.V.C	$T.V.C._n$ = $T.V.C._{n-1}$
1	12	12	12	12	12	24	12
2	32	12	20	6	10	16	8
3	42	12	30	4	10	14	10
4	52	12	40	3	10	13	10

Sum-9.   Complete the following table.

Quantity	T.C.	T.F.C.	T.V.C.	A.F.C.	A.V.C.	A.C.	M.C.
1	90	60	?	60	30	90	30
2	?	?	45	?	?	?	?
3	120	?	55	20	?	?	?
4	135	?	60	?	15	?	5
5	?	?	75	?	?	?	?
6	?	?	?	?	16.7	?	25
7	?	?	140	?	?	?	40
8	?	?	?	?	25	?	60

Answer- 9.

Quantity	T.C.	T.F.C.	T.V.C.	A.F.C.	A.V.C.	A.C.	M.C.
FORMULAE	T.F.C. + T.V.C	(GIVEN IN THE SUM)	T.F.C. - T.C.	T.F.C. / Q	T.V.C. / Q	A.F.C + A.V.C	$\frac{T.V.C._n}{T.V.C._{n-1}}$
1	90	60	30	60	30	90	30
2	105	60	45	30	22.5	52.5	15
3	115	60	55	20	18.33	38.33	10
4	120	60	60	15	15	30	5
5	135	60	75	12	15	27	15
6	160	60	100	10	16.67	26.67	25
7	200	60	140	8.57	20	28.57	40
8	260	60	200	7.5	25	32.5	60

7.6   Question Bank

1. Discuss the time element of cost.
2. Explain Total Fixed Cost with a schedule and a graph.
3. Explain Total Variable Cost with a schedule and a graph.
4. Explain Total Cost with a schedule and a graph.
5. Explain Average Fixed Cost with a schedule and a graph.
6. Explain Average Variable Cost with a schedule and a graph.
7. Explain Average Cost with a schedule and a graph.
8. Explain Marginal Cost with a schedule and a graph.
9. From the following data, calculate Marginal Cost.

Quantity	1	2	3	4	5	6
AVC	60	40	30	26.25	28	45

10. From the following data, calculate AFC, AVC and M C

Quantity	0	1	2	3	4	5
TC	40	100	120	130	150	190

11. From the following data, calculate , AVC and M C

Quantity	0	1	2	3	4
TC	80	102	122	140	156

Chapter - 8

Revenue

In this Chapter you will clear your concepts about…..

➢ *Concept of Revenue*

    ❖ *Total Revenue (T.R.)*

    ❖ *Average Revenue (A.R.)*

    ❖ *Marginal Revenue (M.R.)*

➢ *Relationship between T.R., A.R. and M.R.*

Chapter - 8

Revenue

8.1 Introduction

When an entrepreneur starts a business, "INCOME" is the main target which may be in terms of profit. In a business, when cost is taken into consideration, the other and the most important aspect is revenue. Revenue refers to income of an entrepreneur which is possible only when the desirable output is gained and reached in hands of consumers.

8.2 Concept of Revenue

Revenue refers to the money receipt of a firm from selling its output. In technical terms, sales of commodities lead to a revenue of a firm. According to Dooley, "the revenue of a firm is its sales receipt or money receipt from the sales of a product." A firm produces its product with a view to sell it in the market. The money receipts from these sales are termed as its revenue. Mainly there are three types of revenue. They are:

A. Total Revenue (T.R.)

B. Average Revenue (A.R.)

C. Marginal Revenue (M.R.)

Let us discuss this revenue in detail.

A. Total Revenue (T.R.)

It is the amount a firm receives by selling a given quantity, i.e. output. Total Revenue (T.R.) is the total money receipt of a producer corresponding to a given level of output. In simple words, Total Revenue (T.R.) is the sum of all the sales receipt, i.e. income of a firm. Total

Revenue (T.R.) is gained by multiplying the price per unit of the commodity with the quantity of output. Therefore, Total Revenue (T.R.) is equal to price multiplied by quantity.

Formulae for finding Total Revenue (T.R.)

Total Revenue (T.R.) = Price * Quantity

Let us understand this with a schedule and a graph.

Quantity	T.R.
1	16
2	30
3	42
4	42
5	35
6	30

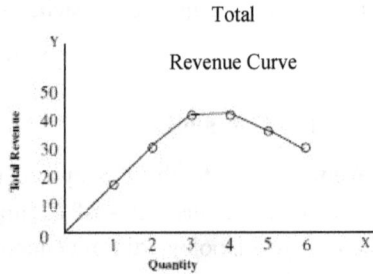

Total Revenue Curve

Explanation of the Curve / Graph

From the above graph it is clear that at the initial stage, it increases at an increasing level. Slowly and steadily becomes constant, later starts diminishing. The main reason behind this is variation in price and quantity.

B.   Average Revenue (A.R.)

Maconell defines Average Revenue (A.R.) as "Average Revenue (A.R.) is the per unit revenue received from the sales of a commodity". Average Revenue (A.R.) is the revenue per unit of commodity sold. As per this, it can be stated that Average Revenue (A.R.) = price per unit. It is obtained by dividing Total Revenue (T.R.) / Quantity sold by a producer.

Formulae for finding Average Revenue (A.R.)

Average Revenue (A.R.) = T.R./Q

Let us understand this with an example: A company's total revenue is 1,30,000 Rs. And Total Quantity produced is 100 units. Therefore, Average Revenue (A.R.) = 1,30,000 / 100 units. i.e. 1,300. This is Average Revenue (A.R.) which in return is its price per unit.

Let us understand this with a schedule and a graph.

Quantity	Price	T.R.	A.R.
1	16	16	16
2	15	30	15
3	14	42	14
4	10.5	42	10.5
5	7	35	7
6	6	36	6

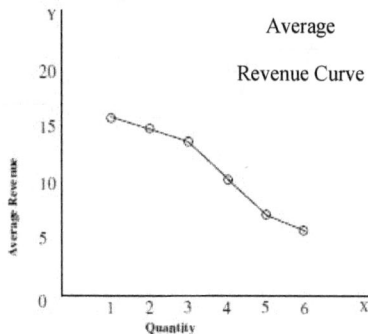

Average Revenue Curve

Explanation of the Curve / Graph

From the above graph it is clear that as Total Revenue (T.R.) increases, Average Revenue (A.R.) starts declines and as Total Revenue (T.R.) decreases, Average Revenue (A.R.) starts falling at an increasing rate.

C.   Marginal Revenue (M.R.)

Marginal Revenue (M.R.) is the change in Total Revenue (T.R.) which results from the sales of one more nit than its output. Thus, Marginal Revenue (M.R.) is the net addition to Total Revenue (T.R.). When one more unit of a commodity is sold, producer gains Marginal Revenue (M.R.). For example, A firm receives Total Revenue (T.R.) of Rs, 5000/- by selling 10 units, and later receives Rs. 5500/- by selling 11th unit in addition. Here his Marginal Revenue (M.R.) is Rs. 500/-.

Formulae for finding Marginal Revenue (M.R.)

Marginal Revenue (M.R.) = T.Rn – T.R.n-1

Let us understand this with a schedule and a graph.

Quantity	Price	T.R.	A.R.
1	16	16	16
2	15	30	14
3	14	42	12
4	10.5	42	0
5	7	35	-7
6	5	30	-5

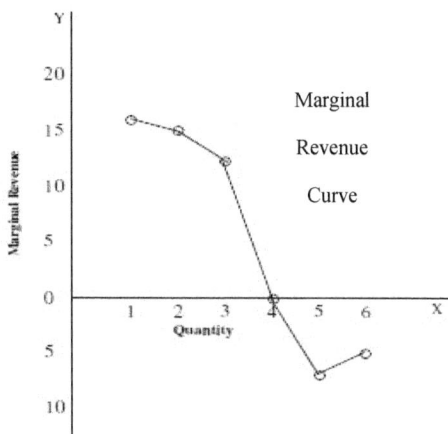

Marginal Revenue Curve

Explanation of the Curve / Graph

From the above graph it is clear that as Total Revenue (T.R.) increases, Marginal Revenue (M.R.) starts falling. When the Total Revenue (T.R.) becomes constant Marginal Revenue (M.R.) turns zero. As Total Revenue (T.R.) falls down Marginal Revenue (M.R.) turns towards negative and slopes downward towards negative.

8.3   Relationship between T.R., A.R. and M.R.

As a firm always intends to earn profit, i.e. Revenue, the entrepreneur keeps in mind that output of the production. He calculates Total Revenue (T.R.), Average Revenue (A.R.) and Marginal Revenue (M.R.) to get a clear picture of his revenue. Let us understand the relationship between T.R., A.R. and M.R. with the help of a schedule and a graph.

Quantity	Price	T.R.	A.R.	M.R.
1	10	10	10	10
2	9	18	9	8
3	8	24	8	6
4	7	28	7	4
5	6	30	6	2
6	5	30	5	0
7	4	28	4	-2

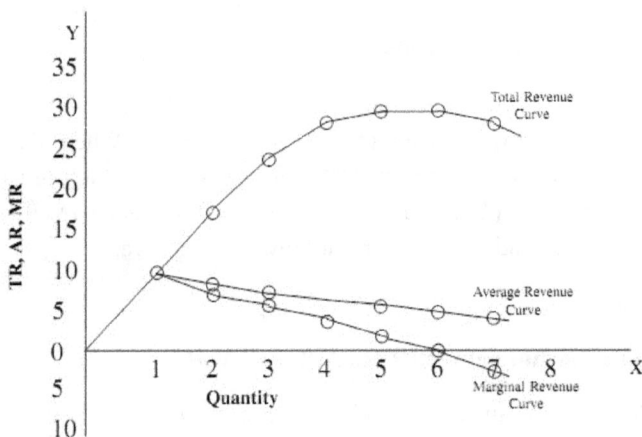

Explanation of the Curve / Graph OR

Relationship between T.R., A.R. and M.R.

1. When T.R. increases, and keeps on rising so long as M.R. is positive. At M.R. is equal to zero, T.R. will be at its maximum.

2. When M.R. becomes negative, T.R. starts falling.

3. When both A.R. and M.R. are falling, M.R. falls at an increasing rate in comparison to A.R.

4. M.R. curve remains below the A.R. curve.

8.4 Question Bank

1. Explain the concept of revenue.
2. What is Total Revenue? Explain with a graph.
3. Explain Average Revenue with a graph.
4. Explain Marginal Revenue with a graph.
5. Discuss the relationship of TR, AR and MR in a single graph.

Chapter - 9

Producer's Equilibrium

In this Chapter you will clear your concepts about…..

➢ *Conditions of Producer's Equilibrium*

    ❖ *Condition No. 1: When price remains constant*

    ❖ *Condition No. 2: When price falls with the rise in the output*

➢ *Short Term Analysis*

    ❖ *Break Even Point*

    ❖ *Super Normal Profit*

    ❖ *Minimum Loss*

    ❖ *Shut Down Point*

Chapter - 9

Producer's Equilibrium

9.1   Introduction

The aim of every producer is to produce that level of output at which his cost of production will be minimum and output will be at its maximum. Equilibrium is a situation from where highest level of satisfaction is gained. When a consumer is in his equilibrium, he has allocated his limited income among various uses in such a way that he gets maximum satisfaction.

In a similar pattern a producer has a choice of alternative combinations of inputs to get the output. He allocates this input in such a way that maximum output is obtained.

For example, Labourer $\Longrightarrow$ machinery.

Thus, producer's equilibrium refers to the stage of that level of output at which profits earned by the producer is maximum.

9.2   Conditions of Producer's Equilibrium

Producer's equilibrium can be observed under two circumstances / conditions:

Condition	Case No. 1	Case No. 2
When price remains constant	Marginal Cost (M.C.) = Marginal Revenue (M.R.) M.R. = M.C.	Marginal Cost (M.C.) > Marginal Revenue (M.R.) after producer attains equilibrium
When price falls with	Marginal Cost (M.C.)	Marginal Cost (M.C.)

the rise in the output	= Marginal Revenue (M.R.) M.R. = M.C.	> Marginal Revenue (M.R.) after producer attains equilibrium

Let us understand these conditions with its cases respectively.

Condition No. 1: When price remains constant

In a market, producer equilibrium can be gained under this condition that the price of a particular commodity remains constant at all levels of output. The revenue from every additional unit, i.e. (Marginal Revenue) is equal to Average Revenue (A.R.) this means A.R. and M.R. are equal. When P=A.R. and A.R. = M.R., it means P=M.R. The condition can be judged by two cases.

Case No. 1: Marginal Cost (M.C.) = Marginal Revenue (M.R.)

Here profit can be earned maximum and equilibrium point of producer can be gained. If M.R. > M.C., this means that additional revenue. This means that producer should continue producing to earn more. **AND** if M.R. < M.C. this means that cost is more than revenue. So, producer has already earned, and he should produce less.

Therefore, a producer will be in equilibrium point, M.R. is less than or greater than marginal cost. He can attain equilibrium only when marginal revenue is equal to marginal cost. Let us understand with the schedule and the graph.

Quantity	Total Cost	T.R.	M.R.	M.C.
1	3	10	10	3
2	6	20	10	3
3	9	30	10	3
4	12	40	10	3
5	16	50	10	4
6	21	60	10	5
7	27	70	10	6
8	33	80	10	6
9	43	90	10	10
10	63	100	10	20

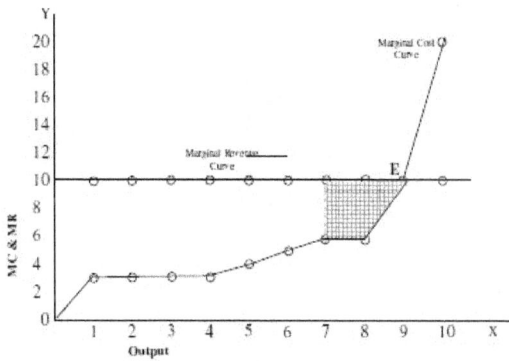

Explanation of the Curve / Graph

As per the graph, it is clear that when M.R. and M.C. curve intersects each other is said to be point of equilibrium. It is clear from the graph that when M.R. is greater or less than M.C. equilibrium is not gained.

Case No. 2: Marginal Cost (M.C.) > Marginal Revenue (M.R.) after producer attains equilibrium

When at a point, M.R. = M.C. the next thing that happens is that M.C. will increase in comparison to its M.R. This is also one level of producer's equilibrium. At this time, price is constant. Producer will try to earn profit by producing more and more commodities. He will try to increase the output to stay in the market, rather than touching the price factor. Let us understand with the schedule and the graph.

Quantity	M.C.	M.R.
1	25	10
2	15	10
3	10	10
4	15	10
5	20	10
6	27	10
7	33	10
8	35	10

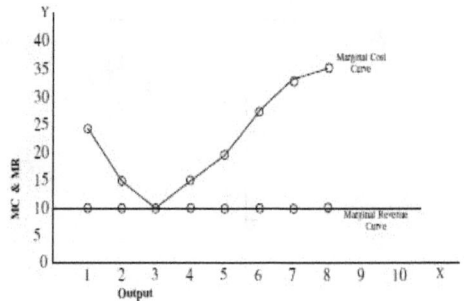

Explanation of the Curve / Graph

As a producer, reaches to the equilibrium point, the next thing which happens is M.C. < M.R. when M.R. is constant, M.C. at beginning starts falling, slowly starts rising. When it starts rising and intersects M.R. curve, this point is said to be point of Producer's Equilibrium.

Condition No. 2: When price falls with the rise in the output

When firm changes its prices towards a fall or is influenced to decrease, the better option for a producer to stay in the market is to increase the production line of the commodity or the output / quantity. In this condition M.R. slopes downwards. Producer tries to target that level of output in which maximum profit can be earned. The condition can be judged by two cases.

Case No. 1: Marginal Cost (M.C.) = Marginal Revenue (M.R.)

Here profit can be earned maximum and equilibrium point of producer can be gained when M.R. = M.C when price of the commodity falls with the rise in the output. To stay in the market, producer raises the production of products when he finds that the prices are falling down, to equalize the profit target.

Case No. 2: Marginal Cost (M.C.) > Marginal Revenue (M.R.) after producer attains equilibrium

When at a point, M.R. = M.C. the next thing that happens is that M.C. will increase in comparison to its M.R. This is also one level of producer's equilibrium. When price of the commodity falls, the best option for a producer is to increase the level of output, i.e. quantity of production should be raised. Producer will try to earn profit by producing more and more commodities. He will try to increase the output to stay in the market, rather than thinking of falling of the price. Let us understand both the cases simultaneously with the schedule and the graph.

Quantity	Price	M.R..	M.C.
1	4	10	3
2	10	8	2
3	13	6	3
4	13	4	4
5	10	2	2
6	4	0	0

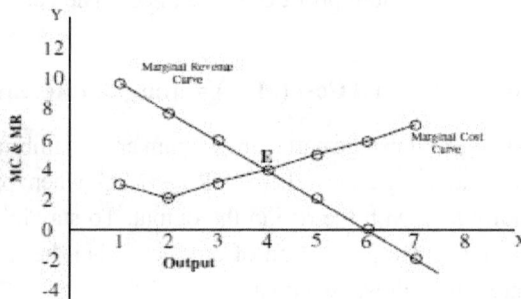

Explanation of the Curve / Graph

From the above graph, it is clear that when M.R. which is equal to price keeps on declining, M.C. starts increasing. When M.R. curve and M.C. curve intersects each other, producer is in his equilibrium when M.R. = M.C.

9.3   Short Term Analysis

In short term analysis, or short period analysis, new company or a firm cannot join the industry as well as exit. But to the producers who have already joined the industry and walked a little, short term analysis is necessary to find out the point of producer's equilibrium. There are four possibilities in short term analysis. This can be clear in the following tabular form:

Possibilities in Short Term Analysis	Concept of the term	Schedule				Graph	Explanation of the curve / graph
Possibility No. 1 Normal Profit (Break Even Point)	When a firm is in such a situation where cost of production of commodities is equal to the income gained by selling of it, i.e. M.R. = M.C., in this situation a producer does not earn profit but does not suffer loss also. It is at No-Profit-No-Loss situation. This is termed as Normal Profit Possibility or Break Even Point in a business.	Q	M.R.	M.C.	A.C		As per the observation from the above graph, it is clear that M.R. being constant at a starting point, M.C. decreases. Slowly and steadily increases. Whereas A.C. decreases at the beginning and then starts increasing. When M.R., M.C., and A.C. curve intersects, this point is the point of Equilibrium. Where Revenue = Cost.
		1	8	6	12		
		2	8	5	10		
		3	8	7	12		
		4	**8**	**8**	**8**		
		5	8	10	9		
		6	8	11	9		
		7	8	12	11		

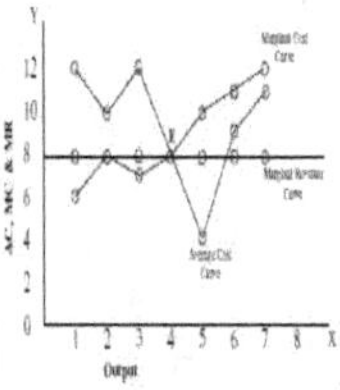

Possibility No. 2 Super Normal Profit	In this situation, firm has reached at such a level where cost of production is less than revenue earned. In other words, A.R. > A.C. In this situation, revenue exceeds cost and the entrepreneur has a good profit margin to gain. Here the producer is at the highest peak of equilibrium and earns profit at the highest margin.						From the above graph it is clear that, in this possibility, at output / Quantity (Q) no. 4, producer have achieved equilibrium where revenue is more than the cost incurred while the producer produces a commodity. At this point, it is clear that A.R. is greater than A.C. i.e. A.R. > A.C.

Q	M.R.	M.C.	A.C.
1	8	4	10
2	8	4	8
3	8	6	4
4	8	8	5
5	8	11	7
6	8	12	8
7	8	14	13

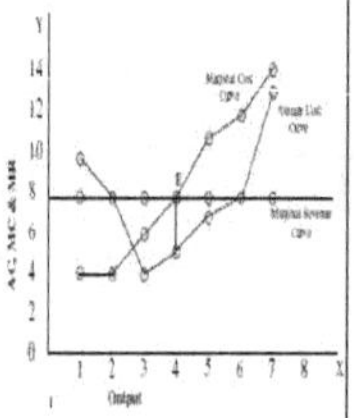

Possibilities in Short Term Analysis	Concept of the term	Schedule				Graph	Explanation of the curve / graph
Possibility No. 3 Minimum Loss	In this type of situation, the Average revenue is less than average cost. In this situation, a producer faces loss as the profit margin is negative. Earnings are more than income.Expenses exceed the income. These expenses do not cover the fixed cost which is incurred during the production. The producer suffers minimum loss at this level.	Q	M.R .	M.C .	A.C .		As per the observation from the above graph, it is clear that M.R. is less than the cost incurred by a producer in producing the commodities. At 4th output, M.R. and M.C. curve intersects each other, this should be point of equilibrium, but due to minimum loss, cost increases than the revenue. Therefore, A.C. curve and M.R. curve do not intersect each other.
		1	8	4	12		
		2	8	4	11		
		3	8	6	10		
		4	8	8	10		
		5	8	10	11		
		6	8	12	12		
		7	8	14	13		
Possibility No. 4 Shut Down Point	In this situation, price of a unit is too low that a producer cannot cover even fixed costs. Cost which is incurred is more than the price of the unit. Income is low. Due to these reasons, producer is left with no alternative than to shut down the business.	Q	M.R .	M.C .	A.C .		From the above graph it is clear that, M.R. being constant cost eeps on increasing. At output No. 4, equilibrium could be established. Seeing to the average cost, it eeps on increasing which is out of reach of the producer. This is shut down point where cost is greater than revenue. i.e. C > R.
		1	8	4	12		
		2	8	4	11		
		3	8	6	10		
		4	8	8	9		
		5	8	10	10		
		6	8	12	11		
		7	8	14	12		

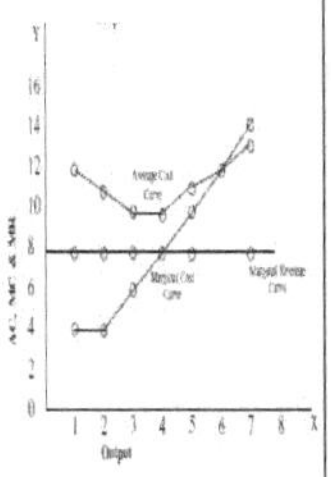

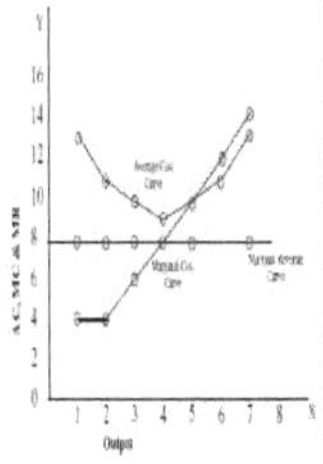

9.4 Question Bank

1. What is Producer Equilibrium?
2. State the condition of P.E. when price of a commodity remains constant.
3. State the condition of P.E. when price of a commodity falls with rise in the output.
4. What is BEP? Explain with the help of a graph.
5. What does producer equilibrium turn in super normal profits?
6. Explain the possibility of minimum losses in P.E.
7. When does shut down point occur?
8. Discuss the short term analysis of P.E.

Chapter - 10

Supply and Elasticity of Supply

In this Chapter you will clear your concepts about…..

- Concept of Supply

- Definition of Supply

- Law of Supply

- Supply Schedule and Supply Curve

- Individual and Market Supply

- Factors determining supply OR Factors affecting supply OR Determinants of supply

- Supply Function

- Variations in Supply

- Reasons for increase in Supply

- Reasons for decrease in Supply

- Distinguish between Quantity Supplied and Change in Supply

- Price Elasticity of Supply

- Degree / Kind of Elasticity of Supply

- Measurement of Price Elasticity of Supply

- Calculations of Price Elasticity of Supply

- Factors Affecting Elasticity of Supply

Chapter - 10

Supply and Elasticity of Supply

10.1 Introduction

The demand for a product will have no significance for a customer if he is unaware about its supply position in a market. Demand and supply are the two sides of the same coin. They are the force who determines the price of a product in a market. The economic theory which deals with the concept of sales of goods and services to consumers is termed as theory of supply.

10.2 Concept of Supply

In economics, when a producer produces a commodity and puts in the market for the purpose of sales, this concept is termed as supply. Supply refers to the quantity of a commodity that a firm is willing and able to offer for sale, at possible prices during a given period of time. In supply, price, market and time is pre determined.

10.3 Definition of Supply

"Supply of goods is the quantity offered for sale in a given market at a given time at various prices".

- Professor Thomas

"Supply refers to the quantity of a commodity offered for sale at a given time in a given market at per-determined prices".

- Professor Murad

10.4 Law of Supply

"When price of a commodity rises, the quantity supplied of it in the market will increase and when price of a commodity falls down, the quantity supplied will decrease, other factors remaining constant."

10.5 Supply Schedule and Supply Curve

Supply schedule is a tabular form of presentation for presenting the data for the supply and price of a commodity. Whereas this tabular form when graphically presented is said to be a Supply Curve. Let us understand this concept by using it in an example.

Price	Quantity
225	100
275	200
325	300
375	400
425	500

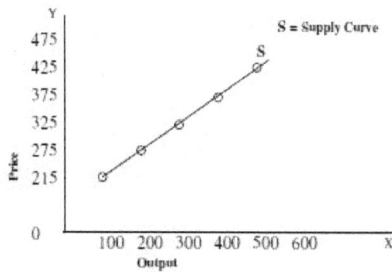

Explanation of the Curve / Graph

From the above supply curve it is clearly noticed that when a price of a commodity increases the supply for that particular commodity increases. Similarly when the price of a commodity decreases the supply for that particular commodity decreases. This line is denoted as SS curve. This curve is for an individual supply of a commodity.

10.6 Individual and Market Supply

The quantity of a given commodity that all firms are willing and able to offer for sale at all possible prices at a given moment of time is known as market supply. Market supply refers to the sum total of the quantities supplied by all the firms in the market by various price in given period of time.

Price	Commodity A	Commodity B	Commodity A+B
10	3	4	7
20	6	8	14
30	9	12	21
40	12	16	28
50	15	20	35

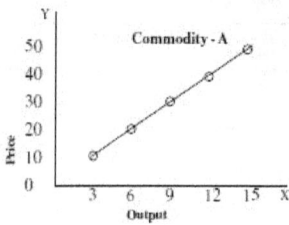

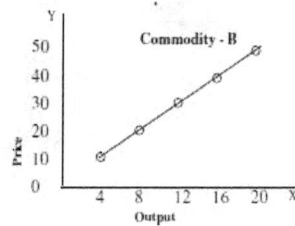

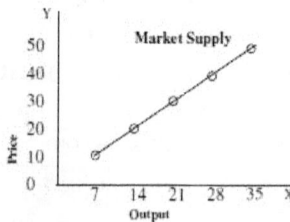

Explanation of the Curve / Graph

From the above supply curve it is clearly noticed that when more than one commodity is introduced in the market for sale, it shows market supply. The line in the 3rd graph denotes market supply line, where one commodity is observed. The market supply curve is established by keeping in calculation with individual supply of the commodity A & B. A graph can be jointly represented as follows:

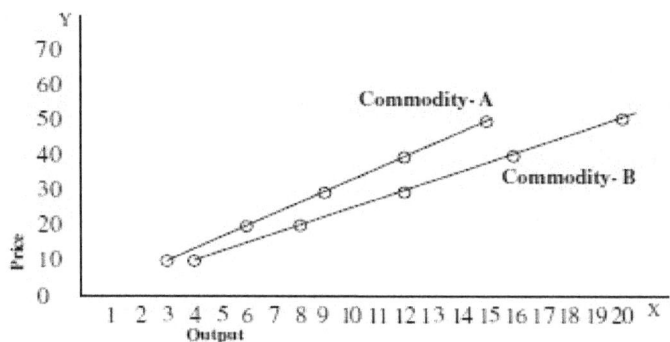

Explanation of the Curve / Graph

From the above supply curve it is clearly noticed that the market supply curve is established by keeping in calculation with individual supply of the commodity A & B. When summation of commodity A & B is done, market supply curve is achieved.

10.7 Assumption of the Law of Supply

- No change in price of the related goods.

- No change in technology.

- No change in goal of a firm.

- No change in the price of that particular commodity.

- No change in price with the respect to its expectations.

127

10.8 Exceptions of the Law of Supply

- The giffen goods will not be affected by this law.

- The necessary goods will not be affected by this law.

- Emergency goods will not be affected by this law.

- Prestigious products will not be affected by this law.

- Scares commodity will not be affected by this law.

10.9 Factors determining supply OR Factors affecting supply OR Determinants of supply

The factors that affect supply in a market are related to firms. The determinants of supply or factors affecting supply can be stated as follows:

1. Price of a commodity (Px)

One the most important factor which affects the supply in a market is the price of the commodity. When the price of a commodity increases the supply for that commodity increases. Similarly when the price falls supply will also fall. (Refer Law of Supply).

2. Price of related commodity (Po)

Price of related goods means the price of substitute goods. If the price of the substitute goods will increase, the supply for the original product will increase. Same way if the price of the substitute goods decreases, the supply for the original product tends to decrease. Therefore there is a positive relationship between supply of the product and the price related to the commodity.

3. Goal of the firm (G)

A manufacture always tries to earn maximum profit from the supply of the goods. Higher the goal fo a firm, more will he supply the units. And lower the goal, supply will decrease. It is the entrepreneur who decides the goal of his company and will accordingly supply the goods in the market.

4. Price of the factors of production used (P_F)

If price of the factor of production used increases, the supply will be affected. More the price of the factor of production used increases, the supply tends to decrease as demand in the market falls. Whereas if there is a decline in the price of the factor of production used, the seller or the manufacturer will try to supply more and more with the goal of earning profit.

5. Technology used (T)

In an industry, if new technologies are introduced, the rate of supply will tend to rise as labourers are benefited. More the use of technology, rise in supply can be observed. Whereas, of technologies are withdrawn, the supply rate will also decline.

6. Number of Competitors (C)

More the competitors, the manufacturers in the market to compete will try to supply his product as much as possible to fight with the competition. Even by lowering down the profit margin. The producer to stay in the market will increase the supply so as his products are demanded more.

7. Future expectation (F)

A supplier always tries to predict the market of future. In his predictions, if he finds that his product will be demanded more in future, he will start producing the commodity accordingly to earn maximum profit. And if he finds that the demand for his product is going to decline, he will decrease his supply to save himself from facing heavy losses.

8. Government Policies (GP)

The government tries to lay taxes for the goods and services which are provided to the consumers. More the taxes and duty; more will be the price of that commodity. This in turn will create negative effect on the consumers mind.

10.10 Supply Function

Supply function means the functional relationship between supply and the factors affecting supply. When a commodity is supplied it is a result, when all factors which are affecting come into existence. All the factors which affects supply are put together is known as supply function.

$$SX = f(Px, Po, G, P_F, T, C, F, GP)$$

Where in,

SX	=	Supply Function
f	=	function of
Px	=	Price of a commodity
Po	=	Price of the related commodity
G	=	Goals of the firm
P_F	=	Price of factors of production used.
T	=	Technology

C = Numbers of Competitors

F = Future expectation

GP = Government Policies

10.11 Variations in Supply

The variation in supply means change in supply of a commodity. This happens due to change in price as well as other factors. Change in supply occurs due to various reasons such price of a commodity, price of the related commodity, goals of the firm, price of factors of production used, technology, numbers of Competitors, future expectation and government Policies. Let is understand the variation in supply with the help of a diagram.

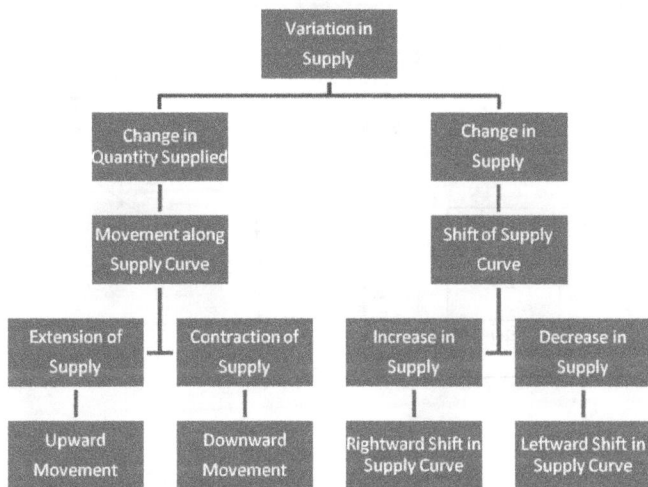

Let us understand the above diagram in detail

10.12 Change in Quantity Supplied

Change in quantity supplied means movement along a supply curve. It states that the producers moves upwards or downwards along the same supply curve. It is caused by change in price alone. All the other determinants remaining constant if price rises, the producer will increase the supply and if price fall; supply will decrease. It is further classified into two parts.

A. Extension or Expansion of Supply

B. Contraction of Supply

A. Extension or Expansion of Supply

The expansion of supply occurs due to increase in prices. For e.g. Commodity A is given at Rs 10 per Kg. If the price of Commodity A increases from Rs. 10 to Rs. 15 automatically the supply will increases from 1 Kg to 5 Kg. Such situation refers to expansion of supply. Let us understand with a schedule and a graph.

Price	Quantity
4	20
8	40

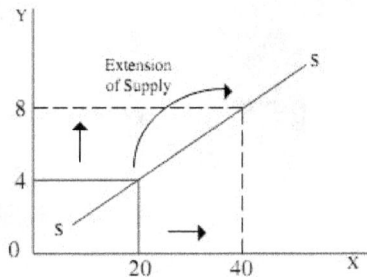

Y

Extension of Supply

S

8

4

S

0

20   40   X

Explanation of the Curve / Graph

As per the observation of the graph it is clearly noticed that when the price of the commodity increases the quantity supplied will rise. Therefore when expansion is noticed, a upward curve is observed.

B. Contraction of Supply

The contraction of supply occurs due to fall in prices. For e.g. Commodity B is given at Rs. 10 per Kg in the market. Now if the price of that commodity falls from Rs. 10 to Rs. 05 and supply goes down to 500 gm, this situation is referred as contraction of supply. Let us understand with a schedule and a graph.

Price	Quantity
8	40
4	20

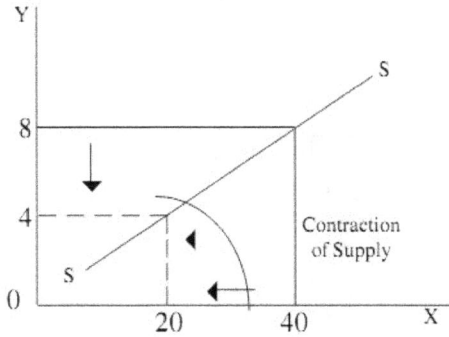

Explanation of the Curve / Graph

As per the observation of the graph it is clearly noticed that when the price of the commodity falls the quantity supplied will also fall. Therefore when contraction is noticed, a downward curve is observed.

10.13 Change in Supply

Change in supply means that rightward shift or leftward shift of supply curve from its original. It states that producers shift their supply towards the left or right of supply curve. It is caused by the factor other than price. It can be further classified into two parts:

A.   Increase in Supply

B.   Decrease in Supply

A. Increase in Supply

Increase in supply refers to a situation when there is a rise in supply due to change in other factor rather than the price. Here the price of a commodity does not change. It remains constant, in such case it is referred to increase in supply and the curve goes towards rightward direction from its point of origin. Let us understand with a schedule and a graph.

Price	Quantity
10	4
10	8

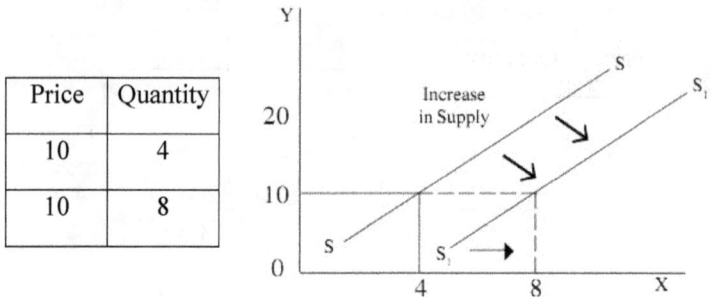

Explanation of the Curve / Graph

As per the observation from the above mentioned graph it is clear that the price of a commodity does not change. It remains constant, in such case it is referred to increase in supply and the curve goes towards rightward direction from its point of origin.

B. Decrease in Supply

Decrease in supply refers to a situation when there is a fall in supply due to change in other factor rather than the price. Here the price of a commodity does not change. It remains constant, in such case it is referred to decrease in supply and the curve goes towards leftward direction from its point of origin. Let us understand with a schedule and a graph.

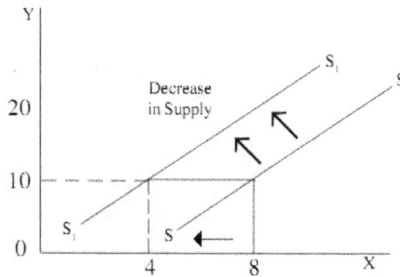

Price	Quantity
10	8
10	4

Explanation of the Curve / Graph

As per the observation from the above mentioned graph it is clear that the price of a commodity does not change. It remains constant, in such case it is referred to decrease in supply and the curve goes towards leftward direction from its point of origin.

10.14 Reasons for increase in Supply

- Improvement in technology.

- Fall in rate of different taxes.

- Fall in prices of inputs.

- Fall in prices of substitute goods.

- Increase in prices of complementary goods.

- Increase in number of firms.

10.15 Reasons for decrease in Supply

- Decline in technology.

- Rise in rate of different taxes.

- Rise in prices of inputs.

- Rice in prices of substitute goods.

- Decrease in prices of complementary goods.

- Decrease in number of firms.

10.16 Distinguish between Quantity Supplied and Change in Supply

Base	Quantity Supplied	Change in Supply
Price	It implies to a change in supply for any commodity due to change in its own price.	It implies to change in price of substitute goods, complementary goods, income of the consumers, taste, preferences and habits.
Movement of Supply Curve	It indicates movement along the supply curve.	It indicates shift in supply curve.
Change	It shows a change in two ways: 1. Extension of Supply 2. Contraction of Supply	It shows a change in two ways: 1. Increase in Supply 2. Decrease in Supply
Application of Law	Law of supply is applicable.	Law of supply is not applicable.
Curve	In this extension and contraction supply curve is observed	In this increase and decrease supply curve is observed.

10.17 Price Elasticity of Supply

Price elasticity of supply means change in quantity supplied of a commodity in response to change in its price. In other words it measures the degree of change of supply in response to change in price. It indicates how a consumer reacts to change in price. The greater the reaction greater will the elasticity lesser the reaction the smaller will be the elasticity. Price elasticity of supply is a commonly called as elasticity of supply. This is because price is the most changeable factor which affects supply

10.18 Definition of Elasticity of Supply

According to Alfred Marshall,

"Elasticity of supply may be defined as percentage (%) change in quantity supplied to percentage (%) change in price"

It is symbolically denoted as 'Ep'. It can be express by the following formulae,

$$Ep = \frac{\text{percentage (\%) change in quantity supplied}}{\text{percentage (\%) change in price}}$$

where symbolically,

$$Ep = \frac{\dfrac{\Delta Q \times 100}{Q}}{\dfrac{\Delta P \times 100}{P}}.$$

After simplification, $Ep = \dfrac{\Delta Q \times P}{\Delta P \times Q}$

The above remain formulae can be understood as follows :

Δ = Delta / Change

P = Original price of a commodity

Q = Quantity supplied

ΔP = Delta in price

ΔQ = Delta in quantity supplied

10.19 Degree / Kind of Elasticity of Supply

Elasticity of supply differs from commodity to commodity and from individual to individual. A given change in price may lead to significant or small changes in quantity supplied. Economics have pointed out five degree / kind of elasticity of supply.

A.   Perfect Elastic Supply

B.   Perfect Inelastic Supply

C.   Inelastic Supply

D.   Elastic Supply

E.   Unitary Elasticity of Supply

The five degree / kind of elasticity of supply is as:

A. Perfect Elastic Supply

Supply is said to be perfect by using elastic when supply varies. They can be increase in supply or decrease in supply in observed but no change in price is notices. Price remains constant such situation can be denoted as, 'Es' = ∞, which is known as infinite. Let us understand this with a schedule and a graph.

P	Q
5	2
5	4
5	6

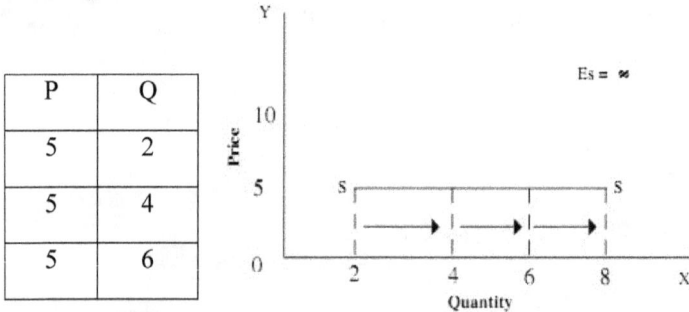

Explanation of the Curve / Graph

As per the observation it is clearly noticed that quantity keeps on increasing or decreasing but prices remains constant. In this graph a straight line is observed which states perfect elasticity of supply. It is denoted as Es = ∞

B. Perfect Inelastic Supply

When quantity supplied does not change as a result of change in price of a commodity supplied. Such situation is referred as perfect inelastic supply. Here prices may increase or decrease but supply remains constant. Let us understand this with a schedule and a graph.

P	Q
5	4
10	4
15	4

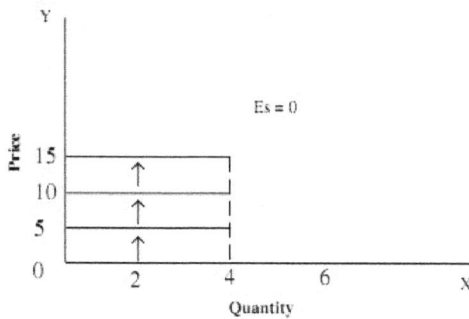

Explanation of the Curve / Graph

As per the observation form the above graph it is clearly noticed that there is a variations in price of commodities but the quantity supplied remains stable. No change in supply is seen. It can be denoted as Es = 0.

C. Inelastic Supply

In this case the proportion change in quantity supplied is smaller than the proportion change in price. If 50% increase in price causes 25% change in extension of supply, it is termed as inelastic supply. Let us understand this with a schedule and a graph.

P	Q
10	10
20	15

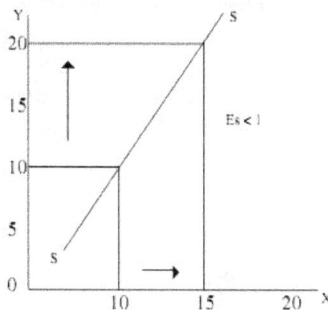

139

Explanation of the Curve / Graph

From the above graph it is clearly observed that more change in price is noticed with comparison to its quantity supplied. Price may vary an extent but supply defers in a small proportion. This is symbolically denoted as Es < 1.

D. Elastic Supply

In this case proportionate change in quantity supplied is greater than the proportionate change in price. If 50% increase in price is followed by 100% extension of quantity supplied it is termed as elastic supply. Let us understand this with a schedule and a graph.

P	Q
5	10
10	20

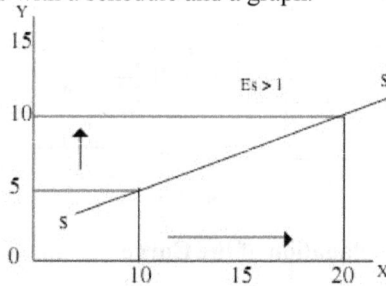

Explanation of the Curve / Graph

From the above graph it is clearly observed that more change in quantity supplied is noticed with respect to the price of a commodity. This is symbolically denoted as Es > 1.

E. Unitary elasticity of Supply

In this situation percentage (%) change in supply is equal to percentage (%) change in price. If elasticity of supply is equal to price, expenditure of a commodity will remain same even when price changes. Let us understand this with a schedule and a graph.

P	Q
5	10
10	15

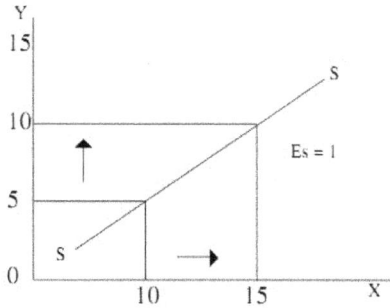

Explanation of the Curve / Graph

From the above graph it is clearly observed that proportionate change in quantity supply is equal to proportionate change in price, here $Es = 1$.

10.20 Measurement of Price Elasticity of Supply

Price elasticity of supply expresses the responses of quantity supplied of a commodity to change in its price. Mainly there are two method of measuring price elasticity of supply.

A. Percentage Change Method

According to percentage change method is measured by dividing the change in supply by change in price percentage (%) wise.

$$Es = \frac{\text{percentage (\%) Quantity supplied}}{\text{percentage (\%) change in price}}$$

where symbolically, $\dfrac{\dfrac{\Delta Q \times 100}{Q}}{\dfrac{\Delta P \times 100}{P}}$

After simplification, $\underline{\Delta\,Q \times P}$

$$\Delta\,P \times Q$$

Where,

Es = Price elasticity of supply

P = Original price

Q = Original quantity supplied

ΔP = Change in price

ΔQ = Change in quantity supplied

B. Geometric or Point Method

Geometric or point method is one of the method of measuring elasticity of supply. In this method a supply curve is drawn to measure it. Therefore it is known geometric or graphic or point method. In this method a horizontal segment on the supply axis is divided by the quantity supplied. The formula that is used is as follows:

Es　　=　　<u>Horizontal segment on the supply axis</u>

Quantity Supplied

10.21 Calculations of Price Elasticity of Supply

Example 1. Find out Q from the following.

P	Q
5 (P)	? (Q)
20	?
15 (ΔP)	15 (ΔQ)

$$Ep = \frac{\Delta Q \times P}{\Delta P \times Q}$$

$$0.5 = \frac{5 \times 15}{Q \times 15}$$

$$0.5\,Q = 5$$

$$Q = \frac{5 \times 10}{5}$$

$$Q = 10 \text{ Units}$$

Now, $\Delta Q = Q_1 - Q$

$\therefore \quad 15 + 10 = Q_1$

$\therefore$ **Q = 25 units**

Example 2. Find out Es from the following.

P	Q
4 (P)	8 (Q)
5	10
1 (ΔP)	2 (ΔQ)

$$Es = \frac{\Delta Q \times P}{\Delta P \times Q} = \frac{2 \times 4}{1 \times 8}$$

$$\therefore Es = 1$$

Therefore it is clear that price elasticity of supply is Ed = 1, i.e. 1. In such type of elasticity is said to be unitary elastic supply.

Example 3. Find out Es from the following.

P	Q
50 (P)	400 (Q)
48	200
-2 (ΔP)	-200 (ΔQ)

$$Es = \frac{\Delta Q \times P}{\Delta P \times Q} = \frac{-200 \times -2}{50 \times 400}$$

$$\therefore Es = 12.5$$

Therefore it is clear that price elasticity of supply is Ed < 1, i.e. 12.5. In such type of elasticity is said to be inelastic supply.

10.22 Factors Affecting Elasticity of Supply

The following are the main factors which affects elasticity of supply:

1. **Nature of Input used**

    The elasticity of supply depends on the nature of input used for the production purpose. If the production of a product utilizes common factor of production, it will tend to have more elasticity of supply. For e.g. cotton, as it is commonly used raw material for production of clothes, supply will be more, irrespective of price changes. On the other hand, if specialized factor of production is used, its supply will be inelastic. For e.g. special machinery is used for production. More change in price will affect supply.

2. **Techniques of production**

    If the techniques of production is complex, the supply will be inelastic, as per the price will affect supply. Whereas simple techniques will lead to elastic supply.

3. **Cost of production**

    Elasticity of supply is also influenced by cost of production. If the cost of production is high supply of such goods will be inelastic. Supply of such goods will be affected by price. Whereas, low cost of production will lead to elastic supply. Where price do not much effect supply.

4. Risk taking

The elasticity of supply depends on the willingness of a producer. If the producer is willing to take risk, supply will be more elastic. Whereas, if he hesitates in risk taking, supply will be inelastic. He will lower down his supply with decrease in price.

5. Nature of commodity

Perishable goods are relatively inelastic in supply. For instance, milk, as its expiry date is very close to its manufacturing date. Whereas, durable goods have elastic supply, as it can be easily stored.

6. Time factor

Elasticity of supply is highly influenced by the time factor. Longer the time period for production distribution and storage, higher will be the elasticity of supply. Whereas, shorter the time period for production distribution and storage, less will be the elasticity of supply. Supply decreases by the rise in price as per time factor.

10.23 Question Bank

1. Define Supply.

2. Explain Law of Supply with the help of a graph.

3. What is supply schedule and supply curve?

4. Explain the concept of individual and market supply.

5. State the assumptions and exceptions of Law of supply.

6. Discuss the factors affecting supply.

7. Explain supply function.

8. How does supply vary?

9. Explain change in quantity supplied.

10. Discuss change in supply.

11. State the reasons for increase and decrease in supply.

12. Distinguish between quantity supplied and change in supply.

13. Define price elasticity of supply.

14. Discuss the degree of elasticity of supply.

15. State the factors affecting elasticity of supply.

16. At a market price of Rs. 10/- a company supplies 4 units of output. The market price increase to Rs. 30/-. The price elasticity of supply is 1.25. What quantity will the company supply at the new price?

(Ans: 14 Units)

17. When price of a commodity falls from Rs. 10/- to Rs. 9/- per unit, its quantity falls by 30%. Calculate price elasticity of supply.

(Ans: Es.=3)

18. If price of a commodity falls from Rs. 60/- to Rs. 58/- per unit, its supply falls from 300 to 200 units. Find out the elasticity of supply.

(Ans = Es.= 10).

Chapter - 11

Forms of Market and its Features

In this Chapter you will clear your concepts about…..

➤ *Definition of Market*

➤ *Forms of Market Structure: Meaning and   Features*

❖ *Perfect Competition*

- *Meaning, Definition, features of Perfect competition*

- *AR & MR curve under the Perfect competition*

❖ *Monopoly Competition*

- *Meaning, Definition, features of Monopoly Competition*

- *AR & MR curve under the Monopoly competition*

❖ *Monopolistic Competition*

- *Meaning, Definition, features of Monopolistic Competition*

- *AR & MR curve under the Monopolistic competition*

❖ *Oligopoly Competition*

- *Meaning, Definition, features of Oligopoly Competition*

Chapter - 11

Forms of Market and its Features

11.1 Introduction

The word market designates a place where certain things are bought and sold. Market is a lifeline of modern economics. It is a medium to bring consumers and producers under a single roof. In economics where buyer meets the seller and carries out an economic transaction of buying and selling of goods and services is termed as market. They come into contact with each other through any means of communication, like face to face, telephone, letter, internet etc.

11.2 Definition of Market

According to Prof. Chapman, "The term market refers to a place where buyers and sellers to buy and sell commodities meet each other and are in direct competition."

11.3 Forms of Market Structure: Meaning and Features

The market is organized and structured as per the situation and circumstances of the seller and buyers necessity for a particular commodity or service. There are different forms of market in an economy. With the following flowchart, forms of market structure can be classified:-

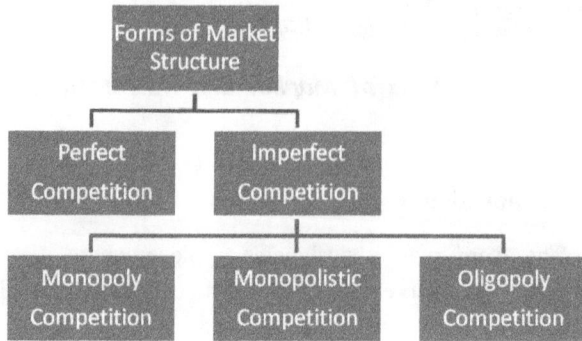

Let us understand these forms of market structure by its meaning, definition, features and demand curve.

11.3.1 Perfect Competition

Let us understand the Perfect Competition form of market structure by its meaning, definition, features and demand curve.

A. Meaning of Perfect competition

Perfect competition refers to that market situation in which there are large numbers of buyers and sellers of homogeneous products. Market is said to be perfect when demand for the product is done by the large number of consumers and supply of that product is done by large number of suppliers.

B. Definition of Perfect competition

According to Prof. D. S. Watson, "In Perfect competition, the numbers of firms are large and the products are homogeneous and in addition to this, the firm has complete knowledge of the market and available resources."

C. Features of Perfect competition

The features of Perfect competition are as follows:

1. Large number of buyers and sellers

In perfect competition, market consists of huge numbers of buyers and sellers. They have to accept the price which is prevailing in the market. A single seller cannot produce any effect on price. In perfect competition, the firms are just a price taker and not the price maker.

2. Homogeneous products

In perfect competition, homogeneous commodities are produced, sold and purchased in the market. Homogeneous product means same type of product which is identical to each other having same characteristics, shape, size, quality and up to an extent same price also. In perfect competition, homogeneous products are sold in such a way that the consumers are attracted.

3. Perfect knowledge to buyers and sellers

In perfect competition, buyers and sellers, both are aware of the trends and the fashion prevailing in the market. Awareness of quality, quantity, price and policies of rivalry firms is observed. Buyers and sellers have complete knowledge of what is going on in the market and what all they will get and give as service after purchasing and selling the commodity.

4. Free entry and exit of the firm

In perfect competition, any firm can enter and exit the market. No legal restrictions are enforced in entry and exit of the firm. Any layman can enter the market to sell the commodity. Similarly, all can be the buyers of that commodity. The main assumption of this feature is price. The firm that enters the market should accept the prevailing price as the firm is price taker and not the price maker.

5. Perfect mobility

In perfect competition, mobility or movement of factors of production is observed. A producer if finds loss in one business, he has full rights and powers to mobiles factors of production into some another business which is comparatively profitable. Those factors can be moved towards firm which pays the highest remunerations. There are not legal restrictions to this.

6. Lack of selling and transportation cost

When in a market, price of a commodity is nearly fixed, firms cannot add any other expenses, i.e. selling and transportation cost in name of extra expenses which are to be barred by consumers. If this happens, price of a commodity will increase and product will be thrown out of market. As uniformity of price is distributed. For this, producer prefers to sell in nearby areas and buyers prefer to buy from the nearest area only.

D. AR & MR curve under the Perfect competition

Perfect competition refers to that market situation in which there are large numbers of buyers and sellers of homogeneous products. Let us understand with a schedule and a graph.

Price	Output = (when TR=MR=AR)
10	5
10	10
10	15
10	20

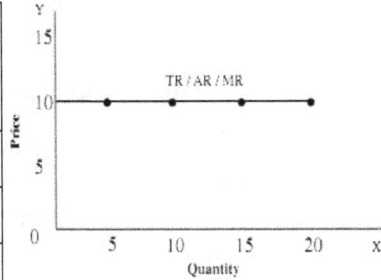

Explanation of the Curve / Graph

As per the observation of the graph it is clearly noticed that when the price of the commodity remains constant, the output will keep on increasing. This shows perfect competition in the market.

11.3.2 Monopoly Competition

Let us understand the Monopoly competition form of market structure by its meaning, definition, features and demand curve.

A. Meaning of Monopoly Competition

Monopoly is one of the competitive market situation which lies under imperfect competition. Imperfect competition means the range or the ration or the proportion between the buyers and sellers are not equal. They keep on varying as form of commodity changes. Monopoly is one of the imperfect competitive market structures. The word MONOPOLY is formed by 2 words, i.e. MONO = Single and POLY = Seller. This means that the term monopoly itself describes it as a single seller market structure. Therefore, monopoly is a market where there is a single seller or producers selling the goods and services. No close substitutes are available in the market. The producer has effective control over the market. This producer is price maker rather than price taker.

B.   Definition of Monopoly Competition

According to Ferguson & Kreps, "Monopoly exists when one and only one firm produces or sells the commodity. In other words, monopoly is one firm industry."

C.   Features of Monopoly Competition

The features of Monopoly competition are as follows:

1. Single seller and large number of buyers

In monopoly competition, single seller exists and looking to the number of buyers is huge. No individual buyer can influence price. A single producer is king of the market. As he is the decision maker regarding price and supply of the commodity irrespective to its demand.

2. No close substitute

In monopoly competition, there are no alternative suppliers. Only one single seller decides the policies of the market. Consumer has no second option other than to purchase this particular commodity or service. Consumers are supposed to accept the commodity and services provided by that single seller; in the condition it is served. No close substitutes are found in the market. Due to this, chances of consumer exploitation arise.

3. Barriers / restriction to entry

In monopoly competition, entry to other sellers is banned. No layman can enter this market. Restrictions regarding government policies are affected. Legal restrictions to entry are enforced. Many a times limited resources such as huge capital investment is need, and no single seller can resist it. Therefore, restrictions in entry to such market are observed.

4. Full control over price

In monopoly competition, the single seller is the price maker and not a price taker. Price are fixed according to the wish of the single seller. A single seller is one who will affect pricing factor. Consumer has no rights to interfere in price fixation policy. Consumers are price taker and not the price maker.

5. Government control

In monopoly competition, entry of a new seller is completely banned, is due to government control. Patent rights are with government. As these rights are with government, no other sellers or producers can enter the market.

6. Price determination and price discrimination

In monopoly competition, as firm is the firm maker, increase or decrease in price is according to seller's will. It is even found out that price differs from consumer to consumer geographically. Consumers are completely aware of this but having no alternatives, will have to purchase the commodity or the service. Consumer exploitation rate is very high in monopoly market.

D. AR & MR curve under the Monopoly competition

Monopoly is a market where there is a single seller or producer selling the goods and services. No close substitutes are available in the market. Let us understand with a schedule and a graph.

Quantity	Price	TR	AR	MR
1	10	10	10	10
2	9	18	9	8
3	8	24	8	6
4	7	28	7	4
5	6	30	6	2

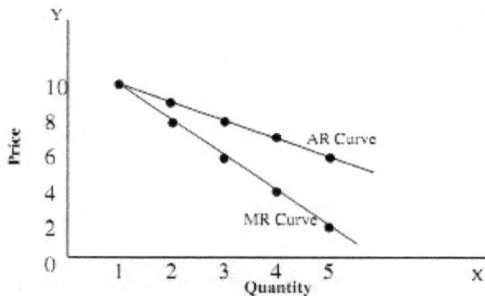

Explanation of the Curve / Graph

As per the observation of the graph it is clearly noticed that when the price of the commodity decreases, the AR and MR are sloping down. The output will keep on increasing which in return will increase the total revenue. This shows monopoly competition in the market.

11.3.3 Monopolistic Competition

Let us understand the Monopolistic competition form of market structure by its meaning, definition, features and demand curve.

A. Meaning of Monopolistic Competition

In a market structure of imperfect competition, when a market shares competitive features related to monopoly and perfect competition, it is termed as monopolistic competition. It refers to a market where large number of firms selling different products under an umbrella of brand names. For example Television. This segment has number of brands, for e.g. LG, Samsung, Sony etc. These sellers are individual firm working under the monopoly and have large number of consumers holding characteristics of perfect competition. This combination is called monopolistic competition.

B. Definition of Monopolistic Competition

According to J. S. Bain, "Monopolistic competition is found in the industries where there are large numbers of sellers selling differentiated products.

C. Features of Monopolistic Competition

The features of Monopolistic competition are as follows:

1. Many sellers and many buyers

In Monopolistic competition, many sellers come into existence with differentiated products. Similarly, many buyers purchase these products according to their needs and demand. Firms sell closely related goods but are not homogeneous in nature; buyers have a choice to choose the best product for them as alternatives are present in the market.

2. Product differentiation

In Monopolistic competition, products are closely related but are not homogeneous. Price is determined by demand of consumers. This demand arises with reference to the quality and quantity sold. Price is fixed, keeping in mind the competition and policies of rivalry firm.

3. Freedom of entry and exit

In Monopolistic competition, free entry and exit is observed. Entry is difficult but not impossible. Entry can be done after legal documentations. Brand name is essential to be covered. Without the permission of the parent brand, entry is not possible. Same is for its exit. A firm can exit the market after the prior permission and legal formalities of parent brand.

4. Selling cost

In Monopolistic competition, where a firm strives to compete, the best way is to incur selling cost. The product is been advertised, campaigns for products are arranged, promotional activities, salesman are been hired, etc are done to increase the sales. To organize the above, cost is incurred which is known as selling cost. But this selling cost or the expenses incurred on advertisements is been charged from the consumer along with the price of the product. It is in-build expense charge to consumers.

5. Price policy

In Monopolistic competition, pricing policy is completely dependent on the consumer's taste, preference and income. Here again firm is not a price maker, but acts as a price taker. Prices are decided by demands of the product by the consumers, competition and policies of the rivalry firms.

6. Lack of knowledge

In Monopolistic competition, it happens that consumers are not aware of all the characteristics and features of every product present in the market. Price preference and habits plays an important role in leading to purchase of a particular product. Advertisement and promotional activities affects the consumer's decision of purchasing a product in this form of market structure.

D.   AR & MR curve under the Monopolistic competition

When a market shares competitive features related to monopoly and perfect competition, it is termed as monopolistic competition. It refers to a market where large number of firms selling differentiated products. Let us understand with a schedule and a graph.

Quantity	Price	TR	AR	MR
1	10	10	10	10
2	9	18	9	8
3	8	24	8	6
4	7	28	7	4
5	6	30	6	2

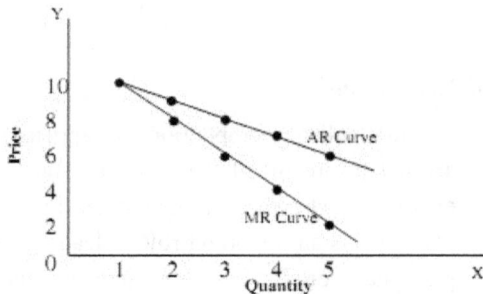

Explanation of the Curve / Graph

As per the observation of the graph it is clearly noticed that when the price of the commodity decreases, the AR and MR curves are downward sloping. It implies that in order to sell more prices are lowered down.

11.3.4 Oligopoly Competition

Let us understand the Oligopoly competition form of market structure by its meaning, definition, features and demand curve.

A. Meaning of Oligopoly Competition

The word oligopoly is derived from the Greek word "Oligos" which means few, and poly = seller. This means a market where few sellers are competing amongst each other for selling of the product. Oligopoly is that type of market where few sellers and large number of buyers are seen in the market. The output / supply and the price policy of one seller will affect the policies of the rivalry firm. In this type of market, homogenous and close substitute are sold but not perfect substitutes.

B. Definition of Oligopoly Competition

According to Boulding, "Oligopoly is a market form of imperfect competition with a few firms operating on big sales of a commodity and producing substantial parts of total output of an industry."

C. Features of Oligopoly Competition

The features of Oligopoly competition are as follows:

1. Few firms and large number of buyers

In Oligopoly competition, few firms and large number of buyers exists. For e.g. automobiles, cement, steel etc. when one firm changes its policies regarding sales and price, rival firms will be affected by this change, and will have to alter their policies accordingly, as they are in tough competition with each other. Firms as well as buyers are aware with the market strategies. Constant awareness is observed in this form of market.

2. Non-price competition

In Oligopoly competition, firms avoid price competition. If they go in for price competition, either they will be thrown out of the competition or might affect their profit margin. Instead of price war, they take up methods to increase the sales such as, advertisements, sales-services, after sales services, etc to stay in the market. In Oligopoly competition, price rigidity is seen and very less price fluctuation is found.

3. Interdependence

In Oligopoly competition, decision taken by one firm regarding the strategies of the market will affect the decisions of rival firms. The decisions are interdependent. Actions taken by one firm will react to the other firms. All rivalry firms to stay in the market will have to follow the changes in the policies taken. Constant awareness is observed in the market. Relative changes are done to survive in the market.

4. Barriers to entry

In Oligopoly competition, entry to the market is restricted as huge capital investment is needed. Entry is not possible for any layman with limited resource. It is not possible to enter the market for everyone. Besides this, patent rights, legal formalities are so high, that it is not possible to enter the market so easily.

5. Selling cost

In Oligopoly competition, to survive in this market, a firm will have to incur heavy selling expenses in forms of advertisement, sales promotion, campaign, promotional activities etc. this selling cost is to borne by the consumers in name of selling charges. The main goal behind doing this is to increase the sales which lead to high profits even after not raising the price of the commodity.

6. Nature of the product

In Oligopoly competition, product can be homogenous or close substitute, but not perfect substitute of it. If the product is homogeneous or close to it, then and then only a firm will survive in the market. Here pricing is very identical. It is the quality and quantity of goods and services which will attract the consumers.

D. AR & MR curve under the Oligopoly competition

Demand curve in oligopoly cannot be defined due to high degree of interdependence among firms. Hence it is indeterminate. Under oligopoly, there is no certainty in the behavior pattern of the producer. So demand curve faced by the consumers are indeterminate. Any change in price by one producer may be may not lead to change in prices by the rival firms. Therefore, the demand curve is not definite.

11.4 Question Bank

1. Define market.

2. Explain the concept of Perfect Competition by its features.

3. Discuss the shapes of AR and MR curve in Perfect Competition.

4. Explain the concept of Monopoly Competition by its features.

5. Discuss the shapes of AR and MR curve in Monopoly Competition.

6. Explain the concept of Monopolistic Competition by its features.

7. Discuss the shapes of AR and MR curve in Monopolistic Competition.

8. Explain the concept of Oligopoly Competition by its features.

9. Discuss the shapes of AR and MR curve in Oligopoly Competition.

Chapter - 12

Determination of Price in Market Equilibrium and Simple Application of Tools of Demand and Supply

In this Chapter you will clear your concepts about…..

➢ *Price determination or market equilibrium in perfect competitive market*

➢ *Effects of shift in demand and supply on price determination*

    ❖ *Effects of demand shift on equilibrium price*

    ❖ *Effects of supply shift on equilibrium price*

    ❖ *Simultaneous effects of demand and supply shift on equilibrium price*

➢ *Simple Application of Tools of Demand and Supply*

    ❖ *Price Ceiling*

    ❖ *Price Floor / Support Price*

Chapter - 12

Determination of Price in Market Equilibrium and Simple Application of Tools of Demand and Supply

12.1 Introduction

When a consumer is satisfied maximum with his purchase and its utility of a commodity, which he has purchased within his income limit, that situation is stated as consumer's equilibrium. Similarly, when a supplier or a producer sell maximum commodities at prevailing price and is satisfied with his revenue, this situation is termed as producer's equilibrium. Likewise, in a market, where consumer and seller meet each other and connects demand and supply, that is, what is demanded is supplied at a desirable price to both, this situation is termed as market equilibrium. Market equilibrium is gained when consumer equilibrium point and producer equilibrium point intersects each other.

12.2 Price determination or market equilibrium in perfect competitive market

When consumer equilibrium and producer equilibrium reaches at its highest level, market equilibrium is obtained. For market equilibrium, three main determinants are taken into consideration,

    a.   Demand (by the consumer)

    b.   Supply (by the producer)

    c.   Price factor

When what demanded is not supplied is termed as excess demand, and when what is supplied is not demanded is termed as excess supply. But when a situation arises, where there is zero excess of demand and zero excess of supply that point is market equilibrium point. When quantity demanded is equal to quantity supplied, market equilibrium point is gained and the price at which QD=QS (quantity demanded is equal to quantity supplied), that price is price determination in a perfect competitive market. Where huge numbers of sellers and buyers transact with each other. Let us understand with a schedule and a graph.

Price	QD	QS
10	10	2
20	8	4
30	6	6
40	4	8
50	2	10

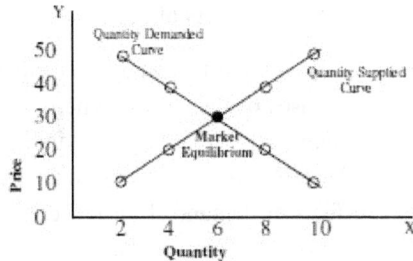

Explanation of the Curve / Graph

As per the observation of the graph it is clearly noticed that when quantity demanded is equal to quantity supplied, market equilibrium point is gained. When what demanded is not supplied is termed as excess demand, and when what is supplied is not demanded is termed as excess supply.

12.3 Effects of shift in demand and supply on price determination

In a market, when demand and supply in accordance to its price are the key factors in determining the equilibrium point, three possibilities observed affecting the equilibrium price. They are:

A.   Effects of demand shift on equilibrium price

B.   Effects of supply shift on equilibrium price

C. Simultaneous effects of demand and supply shift on equilibrium price

Let us understand these three possibilities in detail.

A. Effects of demand shift on equilibrium price

Due to change in demand of a commodity, demand either increases or decreases. When the curve is towards its rightward shift, it denotes increase in demand whereas, if the curve shifts towards leftward shift, it denotes decrease in demand. Let us understand the effects of demand shift of a commodity on equilibrium price with the help of a schedule and a graph.

Price	Supply	Demand	Demand$_1$	Demand$_2$
5	5	15	20	12
10	10	10	18	8
15	15	5	15	3
20	20	0	12	-

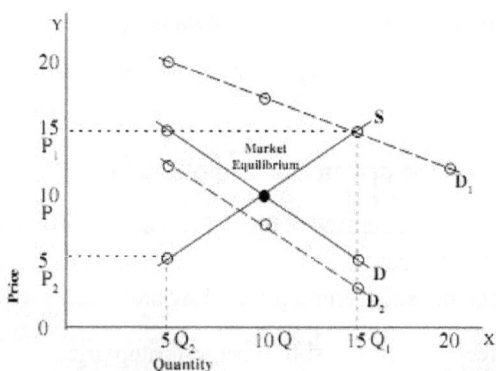

Explanation of the Curve / Graph

From the above graph it is clear that, if demand of a commodity rises, equilibrium price will also rise because of increase in demand. Rise in price will cause extension of supply. Due to increase and extension in supply, equilibrium quantity will also rise. Both equilibrium price and equilibrium quantity will rise. But if demand of a commodity falls, equilibrium price will also fall because of decrease in demand. Fall in price will cause contraction of supply. Due to decrease and contraction in supply, equilibrium quantity will also fall. Both equilibrium price and equilibrium quantity will fall.

B.   Effects of supply shift on equilibrium price

Due to change in supply of a commodity, supply either increases or decreases. When the curve is towards its rightward shift, it denotes increase in supply whereas, if the curve shifts towards leftward shift, it denotes decrease in supply. Let us understand the effects of supply shift of a commodity on equilibrium price with the help of a schedule and a graph.

Price	Demand	Supply	Supply 1	Supply 2
5	15	5	15	-
10	10	10	20	-
15	5	15	25	5
20	-	-	-	10
25	-	-	-	15

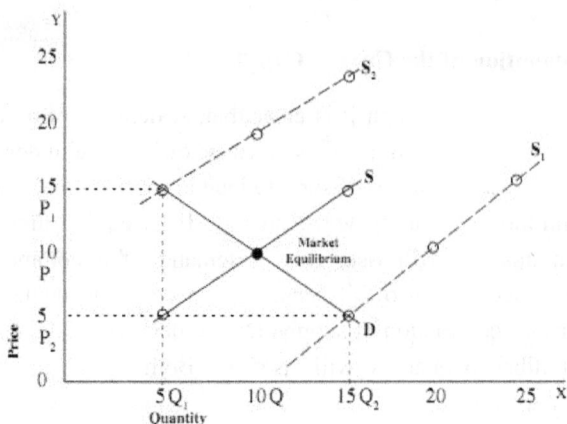

Explanation of the Curve / Graph

From the above graph it is clear that, if supply of a commodity rises, equilibrium price will also fall because of increase in supply. Fall in price will cause extension of demand. Due to increase in supply and extension in demand, equilibrium quantity will rise. Equilibrium price falls and equilibrium quantity will rise. But if supply of a commodity falls, equilibrium price will also rise because of decrease in supply. Rise in price will cause contraction of demand. Due to decrease in supply and contraction in demand, equilibrium quantity will fall. Equilibrium price rises and equilibrium quantity will fall.

C. Simultaneous effects of demand and supply shift on equilibrium price

When there is a simultaneous effect of demand and supply shift observed, the equilibrium price remains constant. For instance, when the equilibrium price is Rs. 50/- and demand and supply of a commodity is equal to 1000 units. Now if the demand and supply of a commodity increases to 1100 units, i.e. increase is observed in demand and supply simultaneously, then too price will not increase. It remains constant. Similarly, when demand and supply of a commodity decreases to 900 units, i.e. decrease is observed in demand and supply simultaneously, then too price will not decrease. It remains constant. Let us understand both the concept with a different schedule and a graph.

170

- When demand and supply increases by same proportion keeping price constant

Demand	Supply	Price
100	100	10
150	150	10

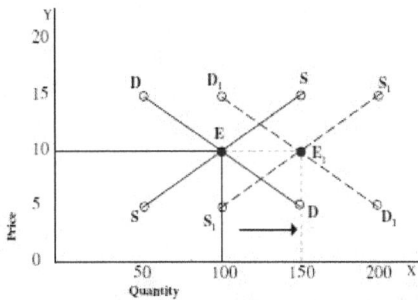

Explanation of the Curve / Graph

From the above graph it is clear that, equilibrium price when constant, demand and supply increase in same ration. With respect to this, equilibrium quantity also rises in the same proportion. As both demand and supply shift shows a positive increase.

- When demand and supply decreases by same proportion keeping price constant

Demand	Supply	Price
100	100	10
50	50	10

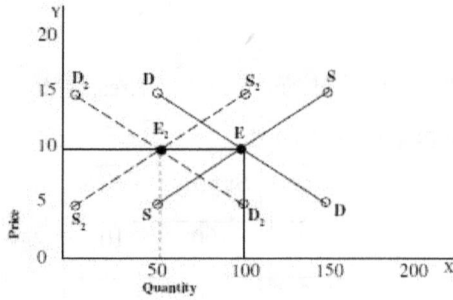

Explanation of the Curve / Graph

From the above graph it is clear that, equilibrium price when constant, demand and supply decreases in same ration. With respect to this, equilibrium quantity also falls in the same proportion. As both demand and supply shift shows a decrease.

12.4 Simple Application of Tools of Demand and Supply

When concepts such as market, consumers, suppliers, demand, supply comes into existence, the most important factor that affects these concepts is price of a product. Price mechanism is highly essential to be maintained. If prices are left free, then chances of exploitation to consumers can be observed. So to overcome this situation, government interferes in the procedure of price fixing. Government tries to form policies regarding price fixation. The two policies that government have constructed and put into actions are:

A. Price Ceiling

B. Price Floor / Support Price

Let us understand these two governmental interference in detail.

A. Price Ceiling

Price ceiling means government itself imposes upper limits on the price of the goods and services. In this government

172

interferes in such a way that for every product maximum price which can be easily accepted by the consumer and the supplier is fixed. Any producer can take less than that price but cannot exceed that price limit. In our day-to-day economic transaction, we come to a word, M.R.P (Maximum Retail Price), this is the amount which government has fixed and in terms of economics is known as price ceiling. Price ceiling is always price below equilibrium price as it is assumed that equilibrium price will always be high.

If the prices are lowered down, demand will exceed supply and situation of shortage of commodities will arise. Excess demand leads to shortage. As supply do not reach the ends. Since there is a shortage at controlled price, there will always be some buyers to buy the product even at higher prices which will lead to holding of stock and then will lead to black marketing. Therefore, government tries to bind an upper limit on price and its purchase. No one can buy exceeding that purchase limits. This will help reducing unwanted holdings of the commodities, shortage and later results into black marketing. Let us understand this with a schedule and a graph.

Price	Demand	Supply	Price ceiling	Output
5	5	1	10	1
10	4	2	10	2
15	3	3	10	3
20	2	4	10	4
25	1	5	10	5

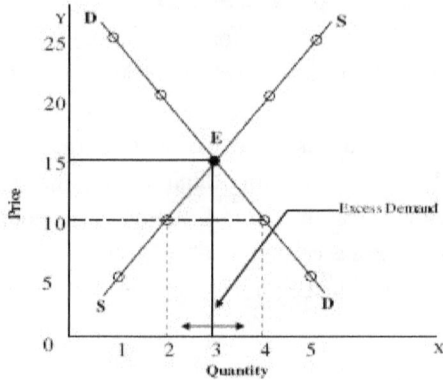

Explanation of the Curve / Graph

From the above graph it is clear that, when the prices are lowered down from the point of equilibrium price, demand will rise and supply will reduce. This fixing of price lower than the equilibrium price point is said to be price ceiling. Price ceiling point will always lie under the price equilibrium point. The excess demand showed in the graph leads to malpractices.

B. Price Floor / Support Price

Price floor is also termed and well known as support price. Price floor means fixing price above the point of equilibrium price. These measures are taken especially for farmers by the government. This step helps the farmers to save them from price fluctuation in the market. By fixing higher price, demand falls and excess supply is observed. Due to frequent fluctuation in market price, variation is observed which leads to the exploitation to the farmers in their income. The cost that farmers have incurred is also not covered if price floor is not implemented. This government interference helps the farmers to at least cover up their actual cost that they have incurred in agricultural activities. Let us understand this with a schedule and a graph.

174

Price	Demand	Supply	Price Flooring	Output
5	4	2	15	1
10	**3**	**3**	15	2
15	2	4	15	3

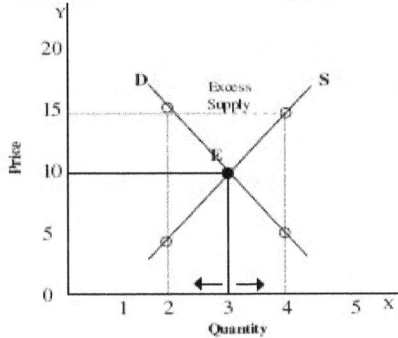

Explanation of the Curve / Graph

From the above graph it is clear that, when the prices are fixed on upper portion from the point of equilibrium price, demand will fall and supply will increase. This fixing of price higher than the equilibrium price point is said to be price flooring. Price floor point will always lie above the price equilibrium point. For this the government will purchase the surplus supply and preserve it, and then release it at time of shortage of that particular commodity.

12.5 Question Bank

1. Explain the price determination in a perfect competitive market with a graph.

2. Discuss the effects of demand shift on equilibrium price determination by a graph.

3. Discuss the effects of supply shift on equilibrium price determination by a graph.

4. Discuss the simultaneous effects of demand and supply shift on equilibrium price determination by a graph.

5. What is price ceiling? Explain this intervention in detail by a graph.

6. What do you mean by support price? Elaborate the concept with a graph.

Sample Question Papers

In this Section you will be able to solve the following sample question papers.

- ➢ *Sample Question Paper – 1*
- ➢ *Sample Question Paper – 2*
- ➢ *Sample Question Paper – 3*
- ➢ *Sample Question Paper - 4*

Sample Question Paper - 1

(Micro Economics)

Max. Marks: 50 Marks

Subject: Economics   **(Micro Economics only)**

General Instructions:

1. Marks for questions are indicated against each.

2. Questions numbered 1-5 are very short questions carrying 1 mark each.

3. Questions numbered 6-10 are short answer questions carrying 3 marks each. Answers to them should not normally exceed 60 words each.

4. Questions numbered 11-13 are also short answer questions carrying 4 marks each. Answers to them should not normally exceed 70 words each.

5. Question number 14-16 are long answer questions carrying 6 marks each. Answers to them should not normally exceed 100 words each.

<u>**Answer the following questions:**</u>

1. Define Microeconomics.   (1)

2. Give one reason for a shift in demand curve.   (1)

3. What is the behavior of Total Variable Cost, as output increases?   (1)

4. What is the behavior of M R in a market in which a firm can sell any quantity of the output it produces at a given price?   (1)

5. What is a price-maker firm?   (1)

6. A consumer consumes only 2 commodities A & B and is in his equilibrium. Price of A falls. Explain the reaction of the consumer through the Utility Analysis. (3)

7. Explain the determinants of supply. (3)

8. Explain the factors affecting demand. (3)

9. What is opportunity cost? Explain with the help of a numerical example. (3)

10. Explain the implications of "homogeneous Products" and "Lack of Transportation cost" in a Perfect Competitive Market. (3)

OR

Explain the implications of "free entry and free exit" and "Perfect knowledge" in a Perfect Competitive Market.

11. A consumer buys 13 units of a good at a price of Rs. 11 per unit. When price rises to Rs. 13 per unit he will buy 11 units. Use expenditure approach to find $P._{ED}$ Also comment on the shape of the demand curve based on this information. (4)

12. Explain Transformation Curve. (4)

13. How does the change in tax on a product influence on the supply of that product? Explain with a graph. (4)

OR

What is revenue? Discuss the relation between T.R., M.R. and A.R.

14. Explain the conditions of a producer's equilibrium in terms of M.R. and M.C using the diagram. (6)

15. How does price elasticity of demand be influenced? (6)

16. Explain the characteristics of Monopoly competition. (6)

OR

Explain the characteristics of Monopolistic competition.

Sample Question Paper - 2

(Micro Economics)

Max. Marks: 50 Marks

Subject: Economics   (Micro Economics only)

General Instructions:

1. Marks for questions are indicated against each.

2. Questions numbered 1-5 are very short questions carrying 1 mark each.

3. Questions numbered 6-10 are short answer questions carrying 3 marks each. Answers to them should not normally exceed 60 words each.

4. Questions numbered 11-13 are also short answer questions carrying 4 marks each. Answers to them should not normally exceed 70 words each.

5. Question number 14-16 are long answer questions carrying 6 marks each. Answers to them should not normally exceed 100 words each.

Answer the following questions:

1. What does an indifference curve show?   (1)

2. Define oligopoly.   (1)

3. Give reason why production possibility curve is concave?   (1)

4. Define Marginal Cost.   (1)

5. Define Market.   (1)

6. Draw A.V.C., A.T.C. and M.C. Curves in a single diagram.   (3)

7. Define an indifference map. Why does indifference curve to the right shows more utility? Explain.   (3)

8. Explain the central problem of an economy.   (3)

9. Discuss the characteristics of Oligopoly. (3)

10. Find out the maximum profit position of a producer by MR & MC approach on the basis of the following data: (3)

Output	1	2	3	4	5
TR	10	19	27	34	40
TC	4	9	15	22	30

OR

From the following table find out the level of output at which the producer is in equilibrium. Give the reason for your answer.

Output	1	2	3	4	5	6
Price	12	12	12	12	12	12
TC	14	26	35	52	64	70

11. Discuss Law of supply. (4)

12. Discuss Law of Demand. (4)

13. Explain Price ceiling with necessary schedule and a graph. (4)

OR

Explain Price floor with necessary schedule and a graph.

14. Explain Price elasticity of Demand. (6)

15. Explain Price elasticity of Supply. (6)

16. Market for a good is in equilibrium. Discuss the effect of supply shift on equilibrium price. Explain with the help of a graph (6)

OR

Market for a commodity is in equilibrium. Discuss the effect of Demand shift on equilibrium price. Explain with the help of a graph.

Sample Question Paper - 3

(Micro & Macro Economics)

Max. Marks: 50 Marks

Subject: Economics

General Instructions:

1. All questions in both sections are compulsory. However, there is internal choice in some questions.

2. Marks for questions are indicated against each question.

3. Question No.1-3 and 15-19 are very short answer questions carrying 1 mark each. They are required to be answered in one sentence.

4. Question No.4-8 and 20-22 are short answer questions carrying 3 marks each. Answers to them should not normally exceed 60 words each.

5. Question No.9-10 and 23-25 are also short answer questions carrying 4 marks each. Answers to them should not normally exceed 70 words each.

6. Question No.11-14 and 26-29 are long answer questions carrying 6 marks each. Answers to them should not normally exceed 100 words each

7. Answers should be brief and to the point and the above word limit be adhered to as far as possible.

Section A: Microeconomics

1. Define centrally planned economy. (1)

2. Why is AVC curve 'U' shaped? (1)

3. Interpret why Indifference curve always slopes from left to right? (1)

4. Explain the features of Monopoly. (3)

5. Interpret the relation between AR, MR and TR in a single graph. (3)

6. Analysis the effect of demand shift on equilibrium price. (3)

7. Discuss the change in quantity demanded. (3)

8. Explain the concept of oligopoly competition. (3)

OR

Discuss the change in demand.

9. State the concept of Budget Line. (4)

10. Distinguish between micro and macro economics. (4)

OR

Organize PFC.

11. State the Law of Diminishing Marginal Utility. (6)

12. Calculate the following table if AFC of one unit of production is Rs. 60. (6)

Output	1	2	3	4	5	6	7	8
TC	90	105	115	120	135	160	200	260

13. Justify short term analysis at producer's equilibrium in following situation. (6)

    (a) Break even Point

    (b) Shut down point

14. Demonstrate the price ceiling and price floor. (6)

OR

Describe the features of Monopolistic competition with a graph.

Section B: Macroeconomics

15. Define Repo Rate. (1)

16. How will you calculate K? (1)

17. How is flexible exchange rate decided? (1)

18. Evaluate 2 causes of excess demand. (1)

19. What is unilateral transfer? (1)

20. Illustrate propensity to save with a graph. (3)

21. Discuss measures of money supply. (3)

22. Paraphrase the revenue policy to rectify the situation of excess demand. (3)

OR

State the components of capital account in BOP.

23. Calculate NDP at FC with the help of following data (4)

i.	GNP (MP)	=	Rs. 40000 cr
ii.	Net indirect taxes	=	Rs. 4000 cr
iii.	Consumption of fixed capital	=	Rs. 2000 cr
iv.	Net factor income from abroad	=	Rs. 300 cr

24. Discuss the capital receipts of Government budget. (4)

25. Calculate private income:- (4)

Items	Rs
(a) National debt interest	10
(b) Personal disposable income	150
(c) Personal taxes	50
(d) Corporate profit taxes	25
(e) Retained earnings of put corporations	5

OR

Discuss the fiscal deficit in Government budget.

26. Define the concept of investment multiplier and specify the relationship between K and MPS as well as MPC. (6)

27. Explain the causes and measures of disequilibrium in BOP. (6)

28. An increase ok Rs. 250 cr in investment in an economy results in total increase of Rs. 1000 cr in income. Find out MPS, MPC and Value of multiplier. (6)

29. From the following data calculate national income by expenditure method (6)

i.	Compensation of employees	=	1200
ii.	NFIA	=	-20
iii.	NIT	=	120
iv.	Profit	=	800
v.	Private final consumption expenditure	=	2000
vi.	Net domestic capital formation	=	770
vii.	Depreciation	=	130
viii.	Rent	=	620
ix.	Interest	=	620
x.	Mixed income	=	700
xi.	Net export	=	-30
xii.	Government final consumption exp	=	1100

OR

From the above data (sum 29) calculate national income by income method.

185

Sample Question Paper - 4

(Micro & Macro Economics)

Max. Marks: 50 Marks

Subject: Economics

General Instructions:

1. All questions in both sections are compulsory. However, there is internal choice in some questions.

2. Marks for questions are indicated against each question.

3. Question No.1-3 and 15-19 are very short answer questions carrying 1 mark each. They are required to be answered in one sentence.

4. Question No.4-8 and 20-22 are short answer questions carrying 3 marks each. Answers to them should not normally exceed 60 words each.

5. Question No.9-10 and 23-25 are also short answer questions carrying 4 marks each. Answers to them should not normally exceed 70 words each.

6. Question No.11-14 and 26-29 are long answer questions carrying 6 marks each. Answers to them should not normally exceed 100 words each

7. Answers should be brief and to the point and the above word limit be adhered to as far as possible.

Section A: Microeconomics

1. What do you mean by Marginal Revenue? (1)

2. State the law of increasing marginal opportunity cost (1)

3. Petrol and car are complementary goods. If the price of car rises what will happen to the demand for Petrol? (1)

4. A price taking firm in perfect competition always gets normal profit in long run. Do you agree. Explain. (3)

5. State the relationship between Average Cost (AC) and Marginal Cost (MC) with the help of a diagram. (3)

6. State the difference between change in demand and change in quantity demanded with the help of diagrams. (3)

7. The price of a commodity is Rs. 50 per unit and its quantity demanded is 500 units. Its price rises to Rs. 60 per unit and its quantity demanded falls by 90 units Calculate its price elasticity of demand. (3)

8. State the feature of Production Possibility Curve. (3)

OR

Explain the Central problems of an economy with an example

9. Define Average Revenue. Explain the relation between MR and AR when a firm is able to sell more quantity of output: (4)

    (i) At same price

    (ii) Only by lowering the price

10. Explain the effect on supply curve due to following reasons. (4)

    (i) Rise in tax rates by Government

    (ii) Rise in price of Inputs

OR

Explain different situations under which budget line shifts. Use diagram.

11. State the Law of Variable proportions with the help of a numerical example. (6)

12. Explain with the help of diagram the effect of the following changes on the demand of commodity. (6)

    (i)   An unfavorable change in taste of buyer for the commodity

    (ii)   A fall in the income of its buyer if the commodity is inferior.

13. Explain the features of perfect competition with the help of a diagram. (6)

14. Explain consumer equilibrium in case of a single commodity with the help of a graph. (6)

OR

What will be the elasticity of supply at a point on straight line supply curve. And How does cost saving technology will affect the supply curve of a commodity.

Section B: Macroeconomics

15. Define BOP. (1)

16. If value of MPC = 0.65, what will be the value of MPS. (1)

17. Mr. A. is a salaried person, what will be the impact of inflation on his income? (1)

18. Define foreign exchange rate. (1)

19. Give two examples of direct taxes (1)

20. India is suffering from the problem of current account deficit.

    How is it met or financed ? (3)

21. State the circular flow of income in two sector economy. (3)

22. Differentiate between nominal and real GDP. (3)

OR

Explain the functions of Money.

23. What do you understand by fiscal deficit. Can Fiscal deficit take place without revenue deficit ? (4)

24. Distinguish between revenue expenditure and capital expenditure.

    Give two examples of each. (4)

25. How can the problems of excess demand be solved with the help of

    monetary policy (4)

OR

State the objectives of Government budget.

26. Explain the process of money creation by the commercial banking

    System. (6)

27. How can AS and AD be in equilibrium? (6)

28. What is investment multiplier? illustrate graphically. (6)

29.Calculate National Income from the following data.   (6)

Items	Rs. (in cr.)
(i) Government final consumption expenditure	1,500
(ii) Change in stock	60
(iii) Gross domestic capital formation	800
(iv) Private Income	4,000
(v) Net Exports	(-) 70
(vi) Corporation Tax	500
(vii) Net Indirect Taxes	0
(viii) Private Final Consumption Expenditure	2,800
(ix) Net factor income to abroad	50
(x) Consumption of fixed capital	200
(xi) Net retained earnings of Private Enterprises	50
(xii) Direct taxes paid by households	300

OR

From the above data (sum 29) calculate Personal Disposable Income.

www.ingramcontent.com/pod-product-compliance
Lightning Source LLC
Chambersburg PA
CBHW060022210326
41520CB00009B/963